Student Survival Guide

How To Books
3 Newtec Place, Magdalen Road,
Oxford OX4 1RE, United Kingdom
E-mail: info@howtobooks.co.uk
www.howtobooks.co.uk

Student Survival Guide

**Lucy Clarke
& Jenny Hawkins**

*What to expect and
how to handle it –
insider advice on
university life*

www.studentsurvivalguide.co.uk

Published by How To Books Ltd,
3 Newtec Place, Magdalen Road,
Oxford OX4 1RE. United Kingdom.
Tel: (01865) 793806. Fax: (01865) 248780
E-mail: info@howtobooks.co.uk
www.howtobooks.co.uk
www.studentsurvivalguide.co.uk

First edition 2001

British Library Cataloguing in Publication Data.
A catalogue record for this book is available from the British Library.

Cover design by Baseline Arts Ltd, Oxford
Cartoons © Colin Shelbourn, www.shelbourn.com
Produced for How To Books by Deer Park Productions
Typeset and design by Baseline Arts Ltd, Oxford
Printed and bound in Great Britain

NOTE: The material contained in this book is set out in good faith for general
guidance and no liability can be accepted for loss or expense incurred as a result of
relying in particular circumstances on statements made in this book. Laws and
regulations are complex and liable to change, and readers should check the current
position with the relevant authorities before making personal arrangements.

Contents

3 THE SOCIAL SCENE

4 HEALTH AND WELFARE

5 MONEY

6 Getting A House

7 University And Beyond

8 Recipes

Acknowledgements

Thanks to our sexy male housemates Nick, Mark and Chris, our parents, the law crew and Peter Hunt for his enthusiasm for life. We are grateful for the help of all our friends at universities all over the country, for their advice and experiences. And finally to the dog, the hamster and the goldfish for all their support and loving when we needed it most.

Particular thanks go to Nick Monaham, a third year Psychology student, who wrote the section on drinking games in Chapter 3, pages 50-56.

Preface

One rainy day in January we got so fed up with our housemates' mouldy pasta bowls and crusty frying pans that had been festering for weeks on end, that we splashed out 50p for individual colour co-ordinated washing-up bowls. From then on everyone's dirty washing up went in their own bowls and we could see the surface tops in our kitchen once again. This put an end to the 'it's your turn to wash-up' wars. We wanted to share this brilliant idea with the world. The book grew from there!

Our aim is to equip prospective and current students with insider information about uni life. Starting uni can be a nerve-racking experience, especially if it's your first time away from home. We've been there and made most of the mistakes so you don't have to.

We hope that this book will be a useful guide to all aspects of student life, so that you – and your parents – can sleep easier because you haven't forgotten your duvet and pillows, like we both did in our first week.

If you have any good ideas for future editions of the book please e-mail us at **studentsurvival@howtobooks.co.uk**

Lucy Clarke and **Jenny Hawkins**

CHAPTER 1

FRESHERS

Freshers' week – the thing you've been excited about all summer, heard crazy tales of, and will probably never forget for the rest of your life. This chapter will help to guide you through the haze that is your first taste of independence, so good luck and enjoy!

Things to Bring to University

- **Passport photos** – crucial for various forms and new identification cards, e.g. NUS, or membership for sports clubs and societies.

- **Fancy dress** – there will be numerous themed parties and nights out, so it's time to dust off that gorilla costume you've been dying to show off.

- **Umbrella** – especially if moving to Wales.

- **Mobile phone** – not essential, some unis may have phones in each room.

- **Map** – try and get a map of the new area early so you can get your bearings. A local guide of 'What's On' is a handy way of finding out the places to go in your new town.

- **Bike** – depending on where you're living, a bike is a cost-effective way of getting around. Remember to bring a bike lock. If you are taking a car, check that there is parking at your halls of residence.

- **Address book** – crucial for staying in touch. Note down all your friends' birthdays too.

- **Bottle opener** – need we explain?

- **Young Person's Railcard** – gives you a third off all train journeys. Definitely a worthwhile investment.

- **Camera** – useful for reminding you of what the drink made you forget.

- **Headache tablets** – if there's one thing you'll regret leaving behind on a Sunday morning – it's these.

- **ID** – passport or birth certificate is an essential.

- **National Insurance details** – you'll need these if you're thinking about getting part-time work.

- **Adaptor plug**

- **Washing powder**

Kitchen equipment

If you are in self-catered accommodation then it's a good idea to wait and see what other people bring in case you end up with 5 toasters, 7 kettles, and no one brings any chopping knives or oven trays. For catered accommodation, it's always useful and sociable to have a kettle in your room.

Bedroom

- ◆ **Photos** – so you don't forget what your Mum looks like.

- ◆ **Posters** – sometimes worth waiting as there are generally poster sales at the start of each semester (NB some halls of residence won't let you put them up).

- ◆ **Lamp** – for study or bedside.

- ◆ **Bedding** – unless specified, bring your own duvet and sheets.

- ◆ **Sleeping bag** – in case you have friends staying.

- ◆ **Alarm clock** – so you can get up for opening time.

Tips from the home-front

- ◆ Get some **tips** from your folks about how to work a washing machine, and how to change a light bulb. (Sounds daft, but you'd be surprised how much you don't know about living on your own.)

- ◆ If self-catered, jot down the recipes of your favourite home-cooked dishes, it's useful to wash the alcohol down with a little food now and then. *(See recipe section.)*

What Freshers' Week Consists of

- **Getting drunk**

- **Enrolment** – be prepared for some long queues, and you may need those passport photos at this stage.

- **Joining sports clubs and societies**

- **Sorting out your room and unpacking**

- **Locating your whereabouts** in relation to lecture halls and pubs etc.

- **Registering with a doctor**

- And most importantly – **meeting people**

Meeting People

You will meet hundreds of people in your first couple of weeks at university and make the same small talk over and over again, which usually consists of 4 questions:

1. your name
2. where you're from
3. what course you are studying
4. where your accommodation is.

These questions may become tedious, but stick with it.

If in the first week or so you don't meet anyone you can see yourself becoming friends with, don't despair, there are usually thousands of people at each university, and there will be someone you click with eventually.

It always feels as though everyone else has instantly settled in and has a secure circle of friends already. But this is rarely the case. The people you spend the first week with are not necessarily the people you'll spend the rest of your 3 years with.

Tips for meeting people

◆ Smile and be approachable.

◆ Make an effort to introduce yourself to the people in your hall/flat.

◆ Socialise – even if you just feel like curling up and going to bed, don't.

◆ If you are feeling homesick, don't stay in your room. There's always someone to introduce yourself to, or share a cup of tea with which will make you feel much better than being alone.

◆ Try and make friends with a couple of people from your course, it's good to have someone to walk to your first lectures with.

◆ When someone introduces themselves, make an effort to say their name in conversation, it comes across as friendly and will make them more receptive to you. It's also useful for helping you to remember their name amongst the hundreds you'll be grappling with. It can be slightly awkward asking someone's name after being best mates with them for 3 months!

◆ And remember, everyone is in the same boat.

Gap years

If you have been travelling in your gap year, try and curb the wealth of experiences you are dying to share. Perhaps save them for other 'gappies', or those 'truly interested' in your day-by-day briefing of 11 months in Thailand.

Joining Clubs

Joining clubs is one of the best ways of meeting new people. Most universities have a sports and societies fair where you are encouraged to sign up for clubs that take your fancy. It gives you a chance to find out about what each club offers, such as meeting/training times, social opportunities and possible expenses involved.

Not only are sports clubs a great opportunity of meeting like-minded people, they are also a fun way of staying fit and healthy to keep that beer belly at bay.

WARNING!

Be careful not to join too many clubs, it may end up being expensive and you won't have time to do everything. There's no need to rush into signing up, you can always join later in the year after checking out your timetable and speaking to other club members.

Sport is good for you

Sport plays a major part in many students' lives, whether you are someone who does the odd fitness class, or a committed hockey player who trains twice a day. Sport not only helps you keep a healthy body and a healthy mind, it's also a great release from work pressures, especially around exam time. It makes you feel part of something and offers you the opportunity to take part in university life, building strong friendships as you go.

Don't be put off if you are a beginner at something; university clubs cater for all levels of ability, and university is a great time to indulge in a new passion. Make the most of what's on offer – it is unlikely that you will get such valuable opportunities in the future.

Team sports

If you are choosing a new sport it may be a good option to join a team. It can give you an overwhelming sense of camaraderie that you may not get doing a solo sport, and is the easiest way to instantly bond with fellow team mates. Many people join sports clubs just to make friends and have a good time.

The stomach-curdling rumours about the horrors of initiation may make you wary about joining a new team – but try not to worry. Initiation is gradually becoming an outdated practice, and even if your university is still keen on the ritual, the experience is never as bad as the stories.

"I had heard tales of having to drink pig's blood mixed with urine in order to be initiated into the First's football team. I was so nervous the night before that I was considering skipping it altogether, but when I arrived, everyone was pretty friendly. All initiation involved was getting extremely drunk so that we'd all lose our inhibitions and get to know the other team members better."

Value for money

Clubs tend to be excellent value for money. For example, we joined the windsurfing society in our first year which only cost £15. This included weekly trips to a lake, transport, instruction, use of all equipment and a thoroughly good time! We initially joined because we were tempted by the sexily-wetsuit-clad boys at the society's stand and we are now keen windsurfers, at a good standard, and have positions on the committee. For some, the wild punch parties, three-legged pub-crawls and skinny-dipping led to some very "close-knit" friendships! Sex aside, we have met some of our best friends through joining the club.

Types of club that may be available:

SPORTS	SOCIETIES
Basketball	Animal Rights
Canoeing	Animation
Cricket	Bell Ringing
Dance	Business
Football	Christian Union
Hockey	Conservative
Karate	Debating
Kick Boxing	Film
Kung Fu	Hispanic
Mountaineering	Indie Music
Netball	Jazz Funk
Rugby	Lesbian & Gay
Sailing	Natural History
Squash	Philosophy
Tennis	Photographic
Ultimate Frisbee	Subjects e.g. Law
Volleyball	Theatre

Transition from Home to University

Registration with a doctor

Another thing you'll have to do in Freshers' week, or as near to the start of the semester as possible, is register with a doctor. The university will probably provide information on where and how to register. It is advisable to choose a surgery near to your place of residence, because when you are ill you may not be able (or bothered) to go far.

You will need your National Health Card and details about your previous GP to hand when registering. If, like most of us, you haven't got a clue where your National Health Card is, then the doctor's surgery will give you a registration form to fill instead.

Getting used to halls

It may feel unsettling at first moving into unfamiliar surroundings, but this is perfectly natural. The move from a cosy home to a characterless room is a little daunting, but you'd be surprised how a few photos and posters can quickly brighten up your room.

Homesickness

If you are feeling homesick, don't worry – YOU ARE NOT THE ONLY ONE! The best way of handling this is to keep yourself busy: surround yourself with lots of people and go out as much as possible. Talk to people, it's reassuring to know that there are others that feel the same. It is a big transition, it's bound to feel weird.

"I remember sitting in my room feeling very homesick and listening to everyone laughing and chatting down the corridor. Even though it was the last thing I felt like doing, I made myself go out and later discovered that two of the girls that had been laughing were also putting on a brave face and were desperately missing home too. By talking together about how we were feeling, we soon felt much better."

The temptation may be to head home when the going gets tough, for a bit of home cooking, washing and general pampering, but try and resist – it may unsettle you even more. Soon you may be so settled at uni that it will take time to adjust to being back home again. We found the moving to and fro became easier every time.

Leaving others behind

Bear in mind that this is a big change for those you're leaving behind too – your family will have to adapt to life without you. The odd phone call or letter home are bound to be appreciated. With so much going on in your new life it's easy to get slack about staying in touch with friends back home – university isn't for everyone, so try not to belittle your friends that choose to remain there.

Leaving your girlfriend/boyfriend behind

Many students begin university in a relationship. It can be very daunting to hear the 'it'll never last' myths that surround Freshers. Inevitably some relationships do not work out, but this may be a natural consequence of leading an independent life with a chance of a new start. But remember it can and will work, if you both want it to. Even if you are now living at opposite ends of the country, staying in touch has never been easier. You have access to free e-mail at uni, and there is always phoning and writing. It could be an idea to purchase a Young Person's Railcard or a coach card which will give you discounted journeys. There are even benefits of being apart:

◆ You appreciate your partner more, and really look forward to the time you spend together.
◆ You learn to be more independent and know who you are as an individual, not purely as one half of a couple.
◆ You have the chance to fill other aspects of your life more fully, but without lessening your partner's importance.

University vacations are long, you normally have around 3-4 weeks at Christmas and Easter, and anything up to 4 months for summer. Don't be deceived by the rumours that you can only enjoy uni if you're single - you can enjoy it whatever.

FLATMATES FROM HELL

Most people experience no problems with those they live with, and many choose to remain flatmates for the rest of their time at university. However, if you are unfortunate enough to find yourself sharing with a knife-wielding, body-building serial killer, or an anorak who's idea of a good Saturday night involves a blow up doll and a tub of Vaseline – DON'T PANIC! In reality, rather than a serial killer, the worst scenario you are likely to face is a cereal thief going through your cornflakes.

"When I first met my housemates I found them very dull and couldn't foresee an enjoyable year living together, so went straight to the Accommodation Office and asked to be moved. Three weeks later (the time it took to fill out the necessary forms and be attributed a new flat) I had got to know my 'dull' flatmates and realised we actually had a lot in common, and then I didn't want to move!"

Give life with your flatmates a fair trial, many of your initial doubts are likely to pass. If you are really unhappy, you always have the opportunity of changing accommodation. You should weigh up the pros and cons of moving, as you won't necessarily be placed in the same halls of residence. Go and see your accommodation officer, who can help you sort out the problem.

ĐIARY OF A STUĐENT

I was forced to set my alarm clock for the early hour of mid-day, to start the pre-ball drinking with my newly aquired friends. I threw on my Dad's reject 1970's tuxedo and I felt ready to charm. Arriving at our pre-arrangedcheap cocktail venue, I was ready to show off my macho prowess by out-drinking my 18-stone rugby playing housemate. This was a mistake.

After several drinks, my inhibitions faded, as did my recollection of the events that followed. I was informed that I arrived at the ball and was escorted to my table, where I spent the rest of the evening – lying comatosed underneath it. I had a rude awakening at 3.00am by the cleaning staff, mopping up the pool of vomit that had been my bed for the evening. I was put in a taxi and made it back to my halls of residence, and realised I couldn't remember which house I lived in. Since they all look identical, I took a stab in the dark at which of the 5000 rooms were mine, and felt strangely confident about my choice. Fortunately I had left my room unlocked for easy access. As I collapsed into bed, I was most distressed to find a hairy naked man sleeping in my bed. A black eye and a ripped tuxedo later, he convinced me that this was not in fact my room. As I was politely escorted out by my hairy naked friend, I noticed one of my flatmates slinking half-dressed out of another house. When he saw me he grinned from ear to ear and said, "You got lucky too!" I grinned back, pointed at my dishevelled tuxedo and said, "Yeah, she was a bit of an animal!"

Ziad Mantoura – *2nd year Law student*

18

CHAPTER 2

STUDY

Unfortunately there is another side to university other than meeting random people, dressing up in gorilla suits and pint-downing competitions. It is called your degree – the reason for being here in the first place – though this is sometimes easy to forget.

Lectures, Seminars And Tutorials

The degree structure is generally designed to encourage independent study, and as a result, you'll probably need to exercise more self-discipline than you're used to. A typical student will have between five and twenty hours of lectures a week (although medics are likely to be far busier!), supplemented by tutorials, seminars and practicals, depending on the subject.

Lectures

These involve the lecturer speaking on a topic and you taking notes, often with the aid of a handout. Though often painful at 9.00 in the morning when the room is swirling and you need a bucket to accompany you to your desk, lectures are a necessary part of university life. Though not always compulsory, it is worth going to the majority of them and taking decent notes. If you have to miss any, borrow a friend's and copy them up. Don't worry about catching every word the lecturer says – note down the key points of what is said and any references to other material. If your notes tend to be illegible, try and write them up neatly as soon as possible after the lecture. If you are a slow note-taker you could record the lectures on a dictaphone so you don't leave out any crucial information. If you know you're going to miss an important lecture you could ask a friend to record it for you.

Tutorials and seminars

Tutorials and seminars are essentially the same, although tutorials generally consist of fewer people, and can be on a one-to-one basis. Both are aimed towards group participation, giving you the chance to demonstrate your abilities, ask questions, discuss issues of debate and get feedback. The class sizes are smaller than lectures and usually work will be set for you to prepare for each class. It is important to make the most of these, as the more you put into them the more you are likely to get out. They may be one of the only chances you get to communicate work issues in an otherwise fairly impersonal system of study, so make an effort to attend them all.

Personal tutors

At the start of the year you might be assigned a personal tutor. They are there to help with any problems, big or small, throughout the duration of your time at uni. If you are unhappy with your personal tutor, it is usually possible to change. You can get in contact with them via e-mail or visiting their office.

"I didn't even know who my personal tutor was until my final year when I needed to see him urgently about a problem with one of my modules. He was really helpful and reassuring, and I wish I had made better use of the system during my first two years."

Degree Formats

At most universities your first year will not count towards your degree, and as long as you pass (achieve 40% or over), you will be allowed to continue into your second year. This doesn't mean a year of *complete* slackness as you may have to put down your results on application forms as an indication of your predicted result. Years 2 and 3 vary as to the percentage of your degree that they count for, your second year could count for as much as 50% of your overall degree mark.

Modules

Many courses are modular and in a standard year you need to complete 120 credits by doing a selection of modules, each worth anything from 10 credits upwards.

Single and Joint Honours

A single honours degree involves studying one main subject e.g. French, and joint honours is a combination of two subjects e.g. French and Business Studies.

Typical class boundaries:

- 1st   – 70 +
- 2:1   – 60 – 69
- 2:2   – 50 – 59
- 3rd   – 40 – 49
- Fail – >40

ORGANISING YOUR TIME

The structure of study may leave you with a fairly empty timetable, which is likely to be less than you're used to. The idea is that you fill up the rest of your time working on your own. It is easy to get slack and fall into bad habits, but if you want to do well, you will have to put in the additional hours required. You may find that the best way of doing this is to work out your own timetable.

"I found it difficult to work in the evenings and at home because of the distractions, so I spent my daytime hours between lectures in the library so that I could keep my evenings free."

Finding the best spot to work in does influence how much you get done. The constant distractions of Neighbours, the kettle and flatmates having fun next door, can be a difficult environment to work in, and you may prefer the studious atmosphere of the library.

The way in which you study can also have an important effect on your motivation towards working. For example, set reading can be very dry and boring (take it from me - I do law), and it is easy to read several pages before you realise you've been thinking about Eastenders for the past 10 minutes and don't have a clue what you've just read. Try taking notes – being active instead of passive can ease the boredom.

Research Resources

During your course you will be expected to research independently by collecting, understanding and presenting information from a number of different sources. It is therefore important that you become familiar with available means of research such as the internet and the library.

The library

It's a good idea to get to know your way around the library early on in the first year, as it will save you vital time when it comes to researching for coursework or tutorials or general lecture supplementation. You may well be given a library tour at the start of the year to introduce you to the information available and how to find it. As well as locating general textbooks relevant to your course, it is worth finding out where other sources of information are, such as journals, periodicals, audio and video-tapes, past exam questions and previous students' work. Most libraries have a computerised search system to help you locate materials. You can search on these by entering the title, author or keyword of the reference you are looking for.

Fines

Books in the library will vary as to their length of loan and some are reference only and cannot be taken out at all. Check out what the fining rate is – in our university, a one-day loan book carried a fine of £1 per day late – quite a big incentive to get it back on time! You may also be able to reserve a book that is on loan.

"I went away on holiday for two weeks and forgot to renew my 6 library books. On return I had racked up a fine of £23.50 which was certainly a hidden cost I didn't read in the holiday brochure."

Photocopiers are another burden on the student wallet, since many books you need cannot be taken out of the library. If possible, purchase a photocopying card, which usually works out cheaper.

Buying books

It is a good idea to buy the most important textbooks – a painful but necessary task. It can be difficult getting hold of books when the library has 3 or 4 copies which 200 students are trying to get their hands on. You will probably be issued with a list of recommended books for each module. It is worth checking out if any second-hand book sales are taking place, or try finding someone in the year above who has the books you need.

Computers

Since most essays are expected to be typed, computers will become a part of your student life, however much you may fear or loathe them. Any databases relevant to your course should be explained during seminars. You will probably be issued with an e-mail address, which you can use to contact tutors and keep in touch with family and friends back home. The internet is an invaluable source of information so get to know your way around it and ask for help if you need it.

Language labs

Language students will also have use of a "language lab" in which audio exercises, satellite television, videos and newspapers are usually available.

Essay Technique

Essay writing is a staple form of assessment at university, so it is important to establish a good technique early on. As essay content and style are very subject dependent and even vary between lecturers' preferences, here are some general hints to point you in the right direction.

Starting your essay

Starting is usually the hardest part of any essay. The best way is to begin with a brainstorm. This allows all your ideas to be aired and recorded so that later you can look back objectively and start to create some order. Don't get bogged down with the mechanics of the essay at this point, just write anything you think may be at all relevant. Push yourself to think of more and more, at least 10 minutes of unadulterated 'thought-time'. Once you've done this, then it's a matter of formulating a plan by juggling things into an order and deciding which information is relevant and which can be discarded.

Drafting

The key to a successful essay is drafting, and re-drafting. There are things that may sound good on a first reading, but there is always room for improvement. Cut out any waffle, even if your essay may now seem too short, it's better to be short and concise, than long-winded.

Presentation

Presentation of your work at university level is of crucial importance. Presentation is almost the 'basics' of an essay, and includes: layout on the page, legibility, spelling, punctuation, grammar, bibliography and referencing. Potentially good work is often let down by carelessness in these areas, which can make an argument difficult to follow and shows a lack of competence.

Referencing and bibliographies

At university level, referencing and bibliographies are crucial to achieving a good grade on an essay, and marks will be deducted if you don't follow the conventions properly. Different departments may express a preference for which referencing system to use, but the most important thing to remember is to be consistent and apply the same rules throughout your essay. The footnote system is widely recognised and involves footnoting any quotes or information gained from other sources throughout your essay. At the end of the essay you must also include a bibliography which is basically a comprehensive list of the books you have used in your research. It must be laid out clearly to include the author's name, the title of the book or journal, the publisher, where it was published and the date it was published. For example, if this book was being used in a bibliography, you may write it in this way:

◆ Clarke, L & Hawkins, J, <u>The Student Survival Guide,</u>
  (How To Books, Oxford, 2001).

Remember always to underline the titles of books in the bibliography and in your essay.

TIP

Try to reference and write your bibliography as you go along, it may be difficult to recall all the books you've used if you've been working on the essay for a few weeks.

NB. Word processing – it is preferred that you type your essays as it shows a degree of professionalism and is definitely more reader-friendly. Times New Roman is a good authoritative type, and font 12 is a recommendable size for clear reading. Justify your margins and include a word count if one is specified. Even if you are not a whiz on computers, it is worth making an effort at the beginning of your course, because in the long run word processing will save you a lot of time (and is an essential ability for most professions).

Check before handing your essay in that:

◆ You have included your name, the essay title, and your word count.
◆ You have made a thorough check of your spelling, punctuation and grammar.
◆ You have checked that any quotations, references and footnotes are accurate and correctly presented.
◆ Your essay builds a coherent case in paragraphs.
◆ You have included a well set out bibliography.

Before you hand it in ask yourself the question: 'Would you be happy to send this essay along with a job application as a fair representation of your suitability for employment?'

Deadlines/extensions

Unfortunately deadlines are there to be adhered to, so if you give your essay in late it is probable you will get a useful score of zero or have marks deducted. However, if you do have a valid reason for not being able to make the deadline (these usually include illness, or loss of a family member/close relation), you can probably get an extension, or make an appeal after missing the deadline. Visit your subject secretary and they can inform you of who to approach. Don't be misled into thinking you'll be given extra time as it was 'your best mate's 21st on the weekend', or you 'went snow-boarding mid-term and are now a tad behind'. Lecturers are surprisingly intelligent and seem able to sift the people who really need extra time, from the rest of us.

Essay tips

- ◆ Researching the essay is usually the time consuming part, so leave your self enough time.
- ◆ Use a variety of sources if you can.
- ◆ Don't replicate lecture notes.
- ◆ Beware of plagiarism – this means the use of ideas or words of other authors without acknowledging them. It is seen as a serious offence, and at worst could lead to expulsion.
- ◆ Re-read the question as you write the essay, it will help you to stay focused on the title.
- ◆ Have a dictionary and thesaurus handy as you write.
- ◆ You might want to leave your introduction and conclusions until the end.

- Use non-sexist language.
- Don't use personal pronouns such as 'I think' unless a lecturer or subject specifically requires you to.
- If using a word processor, back up your work on the hard drive and disk.
- Read your essay out loud as it helps to check the quality of your English.

Exams and Assessment

What a Utopian place university would be if we didn't have any work to do. Exams are one of those unavoidable hassles that impose upon our socialising timetables, turning students out of the pubs and into the library. Exams do not have to be a stressful time; there are ways of making things easier for yourself, so read on.

Revision tips

- Try and leave yourself enough time to revise thoroughly, but if you haven't then the key is PRIORITISE.
- Check exactly what you need to revise with lecturers.
- Even if you work better alone, it is still useful to find out how other people approach revision and what they think is important to learn.

- Never believe people when they say they haven't done any work. I haven't yet figured out why people do this, but it seems to be a general trait amongst university students.
- Look at past papers and familiarise yourself with the format.
- Keep your notes organised as it inspires you to learn more if things are coherent.
- Find a good working environment, preferably quiet and comfortable. (NB don't make yourself too comfy – a mound of bean-bags, chocolate bars, various beverages and The Simpsons in the background is unlikely to keep you focused on work.)
- Take breaks and treat yourself.

Revision technique

Most people have a preferred method for revising, but if you haven't found yours then perhaps try a couple of the following:

- Set your revision out in picture or diagram format, it is much easier to recall in the exam.
- Test yourself – and don't cheat. Or do – it may be the only time you'll ever get a First!
- Summarise the material, it helps you to learn and understand, and it is easier to recall smaller amounts of information which can then be expanded.
- Record your notes onto a tape so that you can listen to it when driving or cooking and you can still feel good about yourself as you are learning.
- Try using a mnemonic technique – taking the first letter of key words and rearranging them to form a new word.

Stress management

Exams and assessment can be a stressful time, so bear a few things in mind:

- Eat healthily and exercise, as it helps relieve stress.
- Go out still, it is important to have decent length breaks, and university is not all about working.
- Humour is therapeutic, so either catch up with someone funny, or watch a decent comedy – you'll feel very refreshed afterwards.
- Put things into perspective – would it really be the end of the world if you didn't do as well as you'd hoped?
- A little stress or pressure can help improve your performance.
- I've never met anyone yet that enjoys exams. Even if friends seem calm and unperturbed, it may be just a front.
- At the other extreme, try not to surround yourself with complete stress-heads, it might make you more uptight.

The exams

Before the exam make sure:

- You know where the exam is and what time it begins.
- You know how long the exam lasts for.
- You have the right equipment ready e.g. pens, calculator, drink, tissues. You may also need your student card to prove you are who you say you are.
- On arrival ensure your mobile is switched off.

Problems

◆ If you are late for an exam you are usually allowed into the hall up to 30 minutes after the start. However, you will not be allowed extra time.

◆ If you do miss an exam then you will probably be awarded a mark of zero, unless you can supply medical proof, or evidence of compassionate grounds.

Exam technique

◆ Work out in advance how much time you'll need for each question.

◆ Read the questions thoroughly and stay focused on them.

◆ If it's an essay-based question always make a brief plan, it is helpful to check you've included everything.

◆ Write legibly.

◆ Check your answers at the end.

TIP
Try to avoid the after-exam chat where everyone compares answers. It is rarely reassuring, and you can never predict how you have done.

Work Placements

A lot of degree courses now involve a work placement where you have a year in industry, which usually takes place between your 2nd and 3rd year. Make sure you apply to several companies at least 6 months in advance because placements can be difficult to organise.

The advantages of doing a work placement are:

◆ You can start paying off your loan, as you will be earning.

◆ It gives you great experience that will look very good on a CV.

◆ You gain an insight into a profession or company you may consider working for once you've graduated.

Studying Abroad

If you are studying a language, you have the opportunity to spend a year in another country, again, it is normally after your 2nd year. The advantages of this are:

◆ You'll become fluent in the language (well, that's the aim).

◆ It's a fantastic opportunity to truly experience a new culture by living within it.

It may be a nerve-racking experience to move to a new country but one that you'll gain so much from. Usually more than one person from your university will also be placed with you and you can always pair up with them while you are settling in.

 Changing Course

Some people do struggle at first with their chosen course, but the problem may be in adjusting to a different style of working rather than the course itself. The best thing to do is to talk to other students to see how they are finding it, or speak to a lecturer who can reassure you. If you do have real doubts about your suitability to the course, then it is quite possible to change. If you are doing joint honours you may be able swap to a single honours course as long as there is room. If you want to change degree completely late in the year, you may have to re-start the following year. Talk to your tutor or lecturers and they will be able to advise you on what to do.

"When I first started my course, I had that sinking feeling that I'd never understand any of it. I was seriously contemplating dropping out when I overheard a guy in my lecture saying how he was struggling with the material too. It turned out the majority of us were having difficulties getting to grips with the new method of teaching, but by the end of the first semester things were getting much easier."

You can normally change modules and it is usually a simple process, but needs to be done promptly. Most universities let you change modules in the first two weeks of the semester. You will need to fill in a registration form to make it official. Don't make the mistake of just turning up at different lectures without informing anyone, as you won't be entered for the correct exam.

DIARY OF A STUDENT

In my first year of uni I barely knew what a lecture theatre was. My work paled into insignificance as I concentrated my time on liver destruction. I somehow managed to get by with my work, and was only called up to the Dean of Students' Office once for absence. I was always busy at uni, my usual routine consisting of getting up at mid-day, watching kids TV, eating dinner, and then it was time to start drinking again. It's surprising how quickly days whiz by when you have such an exciting lifestyle. I didn't even notice the lack of work I was doing. Before I realised it, it was exam time – and to be quite frank, I was buggered. Needless to say, I didn't scrape the 40% I needed. Whilst at the time it didn't seem the biggest problem as it didn't count towards my final degree, the consequences raised their ugly head later, when I had to return home a month early from Morocco to take my re-sits. My advice is to make the most of your first year, but remember that study is a major part of university, and it's wise to get into good habits early on.

Alice Flynn – *2nd year English Literature*

CHAPTER

3

THE SOCIAL SCENE

The availability of cheap alcohol combined with thousands of like-minded students newly released from home may provide a licence to party 24/7, as all hopes of getting a degree fade slowly into the distance. The social side of university will probably provide you with some of your most memorable experiences. While it's important to make the most of them, remember that you only have one shot at a degree, one liver and a limited supply of expendable brain cells.

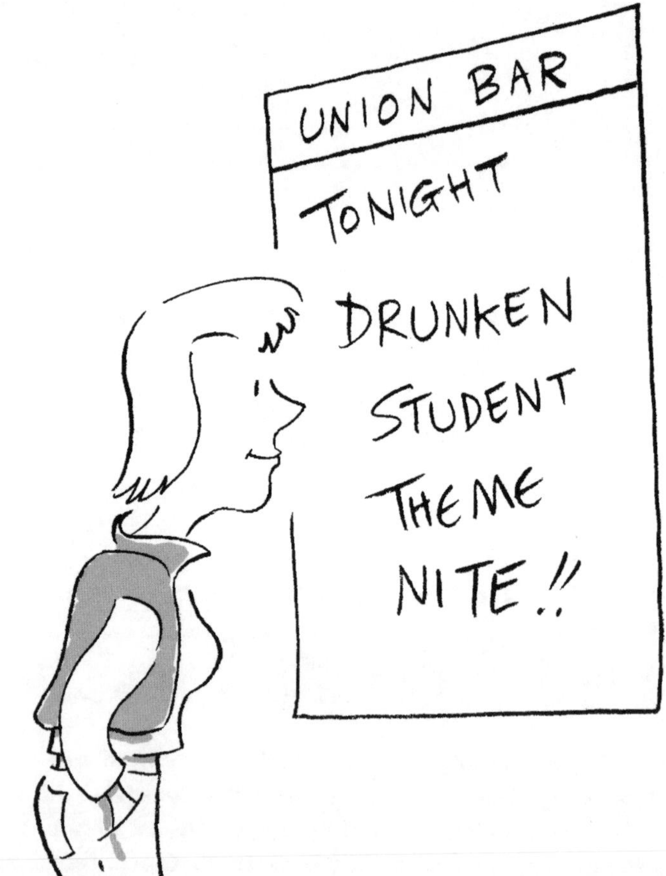
UNION BAR
TONIGHT
DRUNKEN
STUDENT
THEME
NITE !!

Union Entertainment

No matter how diverse your socialising tastes are you're bound to find your niche somewhere. The combination of the student union and the opportunities available in your local town/city are likely to leave you with a busy social calendar.

Because the student union is specifically designed to cater for impoverished students, alcohol and entry prices are often cheaper than most venues in town.

Live music

Students have the opportunity to see a huge range of live music as student towns draw the best of national talent to their doorsteps. Big bands regularly tour student unions, but you will also get the chance to see up and coming bands – the stars of tomorrow at very cheap prices. It's a great opportunity to broaden your music tastes without excessive cost.

Comedy and film nights

A lot of comedians gig at universities and colleges. If you go to a uni with a large student population there is a fair chance that big name comics will feature at some point – keep your eyes peeled for posters.

Unions often show films on a big screen, providing a cheap way to see things you missed first time round.

Themed nights

Find out the entertainment timetable for what's going on in your union – you can usually pick up free wall charts or leaflets for the month's events. It is likely that there will be a regular schedule of themes for the main bar. Different nights play different music and have various drinks promotions and you'll probably start getting into a routine of knowing which nights to go out and which nights to stay in watching the box. There are always the calendar events such as Christmas and Halloween parties, and then of course the themed nights which may include anything from Porn Star parties, Cowboys and Indians, Saucy Uniforms, Bond nights, Hawaiian and Traffic Light parties (where you wear red, orange, or green depending on if you are single or available). Whatever the theme, the main objective is for everyone to dress as scantily as possible. You will inevitably need your union card to get in and take part in all of the above. Non-members will need signing in by a member, usually at a small cost.

Town/City Entertainment

The best ways to find out what's going on in your university town are through asking other students, looking up events in the local paper and keeping an eye out for posters or flyers. Experiment and try out some new places you wouldn't normally venture into.

Here are some ideas of things to do:

Big nights

◆ **Clubbing.** The music in clubs will be very diverse depending on the venue. As a general rule though commercial house and garage usually take centre stage on weekends, and funk and hip-hop nights tend to be found mid-week. Check the dress code in advance – trainers may not be allowed and men may have to wear shirts on Fridays or Saturdays.

"We always avoid town on weekends as entry prices are really high and the queues are massive."

◆ **Pub crawls**. It can be difficult to move everyone from pub to pub so plan out the route and make sure people know where the next watering hole is.

◆ **Live music**. At some point try and take advantage of the live music available – there's always something to suit everyone's tastes.

Quiet nights

◆ **Theatre.** There is more to theatre than Shakespeare. There are hundreds of interesting productions going on locally so make the most of your student discount and go and see them.

◆ **Cinema.** You can use your NUS Mondays to Thursdays for discount.

- ◆ **Coffee houses**. Most are open in the evening, and it's a good way to catch up with people over a drink, but minus the hangover in the morning.

- ◆ **Karaoke.** Gives the prima donnas of uni the chance to show off their favourite hits in front of cloth-eared drunks.

- ◆ **Bowling/Ice-skating/Quaser Laser.** A bit old-skool, but still plenty of fun.

House parties

If none of the above floats your boat, you can always create your own alternative by throwing a house party.

Pros of throwing a house party:
- ◆ If it's a success you'll be remembered as 'the person that threw that legendary party'.
- ◆ It is your chance to select the people you want to socialise with – especially those fit boys/girls you've had your eye on all year.

Cons of throwing a house party:
- ◆ The stress and hassle of being the organiser.
- ◆ The expense – people will inevitably eat your food, drink your alcohol and generally damage everything worth anything.
- ◆ You may not know everyone that comes through the door and things may get stolen.

♦ The morning after the night before: the puke plastered bathroom, the alcohol stained carpet and the abyss of cans and bottles that will re-appear for the next 6 weeks.

TIPS

If you are still crazy enough to go ahead with it, here are some tips to help:

♦ Make sure everyone in your house agrees to it.

♦ Lock expensive things away.

♦ Record CDs onto tape as they could get scratched or stolen.

♦ If you are going the whole hog, think about having themed rooms to suit individuals, for example, a chill out room, dance room and love shack.

♦ Have drinks in the kitchen or on an easily wipeable surface.

♦ Put bin bags in each room as it makes the clean up a little easier.

♦ Have cloths etc. on stand-by.

♦ If someone spills red wine, pour white wine straight over the top and leave it till the colour changes. It may sound bizarre, but trust us, it works.

♦ Put out food you want to be eaten, otherwise people will delve into your cupboards in those hungry 2.00am fridge raids.

♦ Have the toilet clearly signed so people don't pee on your sofa or in your flowerpots.

♦ Don't announce your party in the union on a busy night or else there could be a lot of unwanted randomers arriving.

"Don't put your beer in the fridge if you want to see it again, because all's fair in love, war and parties."

Drinking Games

Nick Monaham, 3rd year Psychology student and expert in drinking games writes:

Drinking games often receive a bad press, being associated with the rugby club mentality, or simply no mentality at all. Much of this poor reputation can be attributed to misunderstanding – drinking games are very versatile and varied and can be easily adjusted to suit the needs of those involved. In this section I introduce a range of universal rules for drinking games, and explain how to play a number of my favourites. No doubt many of you, as you read it, will ridicule me for not knowing other rules or apparently getting them wrong. Please acknowledge that the beauty of drinking games is that they are infinitely varied.

Universal drinking laws

Fines

There are certain rules to drinking games that ought to be observed. Firstly the question of fines must be explained. Principally, whenever a person makes a mistake, in accordance with the established rules of the game, a fine is taken. A two-finger measure, against the side of the drinking receptacle, is the standard fine. At certain significant points, a larger amount may be drunk, such as a full pint, or whatever remains in the guilty party's glass. Clearly these fines need to be predetermined, based upon factors such as the strength of drink, likelihood of mistakes, alcohol tolerance of players etc.

Names

Serious players, attempting to instil a degree of organisation to the proceedings may desire to nominate a 'Chief', and possibly a Deputy. These two individuals are addressed by the appropriate titles at all times, and any failure to do so earns the culprit a fine. The Chief and Deputy are also those people who know all the games, enjoy enforcing them on others, and hide behind their self-imposed authority to avoid being stitched themselves. Don't become frustrated with their autocracy – their size normally indicates that they have a wealth of drinking experience, and could heavily out-drink you if they really had to.

Pointing

It is a universal law in drinking games that no pointing with a finger is allowed within the drinking circle. Instead, players must 'point' to others, or indicate the direction of play, with their elbow or limb/joint of their choice. Failure to do so results in the inevitable.

Swearing

Any swearing must be accompanied with that infuriating and clichéd 'inverted commas' finger gesture. This rule is virtually impossible to adhere to.

Drinking hands

A particular gem of a rule, that is well worth applying, is that all players must only drink using a particular hand. This could be the left hand all night, change with each game, or even be determined by the side of the clockface which the minute hand is on at that time. However vigilant or sober you are, or how many others you catch out, you are sure to slip up yourself at some point. Particular derision is given to those who are fined for failing to abide by this rule, and then proceed to consume the resulting fine with the same wrong hand.

False accusation

Wrongly accusing any player of breaking the rules, when they in fact have not, results in the false accuser undertaking a fine.

A further set of rules, separate from the specific game being played, can be adopted to add to the tactical intrigue and level of consumption within the drinking circle. Unfortunately for some, they also test perception and reaction times and a less than sharp player can find themselves caught in a vicious circle of error-induced drinking:

Thumbmaster

One player is nominated as 'thumbmaster'. At any stage during the game this person may place (preferably subtly) one thumb onto the edge of the table. Other players need to spot this and do exactly as the thumbmaster has done. The last player to do so collects the necessary award, and becomes the new thumbmaster – and so it continues.

Mr Freeze

Essentially the same format as thumbmaster. The nominated player, as inconspicuously or as exuberantly as they desire, adopts a pose which they hold until one dozy b..... has still to notice that everyone else has one finger up their nose and the other in the crotch of the person next to them.

Golf ball/coin

Slightly different is the use of a golf ball, single coin, or other such item within the drinking circle. The person in possession of the all important item is allowed to drop it into the drink of any other person of their choice. Having allowed their defences to falter, the now unfortunate owner of the item has to retrieve it from their glass, when it has been emptied (referred to as "rescuing the Queen" in the case of a coin). The only comfort to this individual is that they are now in possession of the item, and can dispose of it as they see fit.

Games

Twenty-one
You may find this game a good initiation to drinking games, due to its simplicity, and is often played by experienced players as a mental and physical warm-up.

Players are seated in a circle (as with virtually all games).

One person starts the game by saying the number 1, and indicating the direction in which the game is to move around the circle (e.g. To my left, 1) – remember no pointing.

The adjacent player, in the indicated direction would then say 2. Essentially, the circle counts to 21.

Unless 2 years old, or totally comatosed, further rules are added to get the juices flowing.

Each player, on his turn, must say either 1 number, or 2 or 3 consecutive numbers (e.g. 14, 15, 16).

If the preceding player says
1 number ☛ turn moves to adjacent player
2 numbers ☛ game changes direction
3 numbers ☛ same direction, but turn skips one person in circle.

No player may say the same amount of numbers as the previous player, with the exception of 1 number. Therefore, if the player before said 2 numbers (7,8), you could not then say just 9,10.

Beyond the number 15 or so, players need to correctly judge the right amount of numbers they should say in order to land the number 21 on a particular person, or at least not on their own turn. The person who 21 does land on is requested to draw the round to a conclusion and see off their drink.

A compensatory privilege is that they may then choose any number they wish to be replaced by a phrase/action of their choice. This so-called number replacement is to be strictly adhered to in all subsequent rounds. As the number of rounds increases, a growing amount of numbers have elaborate replacements, and hence the game grows in complexity.

"It was remarkable how long we were allowed to stay in one venue, considering someone was standing up and shouting '13, the barman's mother is a Bavarian swamp donkey, 15'!"

Verdict

'The archetypal drinking game.'
'Essential knowledge for any human being.'

Nick Farr Jones

This is without doubt my favourite drinking game. The best way to describe how to play it would be as follows:

Remind yourself of 21, and the basic concept of counting up as the game moves around the circle.

Add to that the replacement of the conventional numbers, with Roman numerals (i.e. 1,2,3,4 would be I, II, III, IV etc.).

Add to that the replacement of I, V X with Nick, Farr and Jones respectively (former Australian Rugby Union captain).

Take away the skipping, and changing direction of 21 (unless you are exceptionally crazy!).

Therefore, each player says only 1 number, and the game continues in the same direction.

1 to 5 would be:

> 1 = "Nick"
> 2 = "Nick, Nick"
> 3 = "Nick, Nick, Nick"
> 4 = "Nick, Farr"
> 5 = "Farr"

Significant pauses/hesitation or blatant mistakes result in the mandatory fine.

After each mistake, the guilty party starts the counting again, from 1 (Nick).

Verdict

'There's always someone totally incapable of converting numbers to numerals, let alone Nick, Farr and Jones.'
'Highest number known to have been reached was 39 (Jones Jones Jones Nick Jones), set by members of the University of Wales Air Squadron.'
'Not very common, but a joy to play.'

1 Up, 1 Down

One particular breed of drinking games could be described as "Thinking Man's Games". Involving a degree of lateral thinking, such games essentially require players to work out the rules themselves!

At least 1, but preferably several (particularly in large circles) of the players need to know the rules.

One of them explains to the other players that, on their turn, they are required to say one of only 3 things:

> 2 up
>
> 2 down or
>
> 1 up, 1 down

They will then explain that they will tell each person, on their turn, whether they have said the right thing. If they haven't then a fine is expected to be consumed. Those who know the rules must always answer correctly.

Based on this, naïve players are told that they need to figure out the rule which dictates which of the three statements they should say.

Before you become overwhelmingly confused, or to rescue you if you already are, I shall explain what each of the 3 statements refers to.

To correctly respond, according to the rule, players must say the statement which refers to the **position of their hands.**

Therefore, if both hands are high, in relation to their body – such as scratching their head with one, smoking with the other – then they would say "2 up". Similarly, if their hands were in their lap, they would say "2 down".

The game proceeds around the circle, each person issuing their latest guess as to the correct statement.

The total bemusement which is induced is wonderful to watch, as players may coincidentally say the correct statement, whilst not having a Scooby why they got it right. Alternatively, others are convinced they have worked out the rule, only to discover to their cost that they didn't in fact know it at all, when it comes to their turn. Those in the know can subtly mislead other players, disguising the significance of their hand positions, and fuelling players' theories about the statements following some sort of pattern, or being based on the statement before.

The only other type of this game which I can think of involves each player saying "I like…, but I don't like…". The word they describe as liking must contain a double letter (e.g. "tt"), whilst the item which they don't like must not. For example, "I like football, but I don't like rugby" would be a valid statement.

Verdict

'Another excellent warm-up game.'
'High comedy value.'
'Some people just never get it!'

Sports Games

A big sporting occasion is often eagerly awaited by sports fans and off-licences alike. The most effective way to remember key moments in a match, and significantly enhance your enjoyment of it, is to closely entwine mankind's 2 greatest inventions – sport and alcohol. Drinking games can be made to fit any match of whatever sport. Let us take England v Scotland in the 6 Nations Championship in 2000. Each spectator present around the television picks the name of a player from a hat. This player may become both their sporting hero, yet their drinking downfall! Whenever the sporting player touches the ball, the relevant drinking player sips their drink. If the player scores, the corresponding player has to finish their drink. The infuriating defeat of the English that day wasn't such a sombre occasion as it could have been, without the presence of a friend of mine called Mrs. S. Artois.

Verdict

'Another infinitely variable/flexible game.'
'Monitor drinking throughout – hooliganism is not condoned!'

Phew! Thank you Nick. To modify an age-old saying, experience is worth a thousand words. This section can provide little more than an insightful guide into the fundamentals of drinking games, and hopefully allay any apprehensions which you may have. However, the only way to learn the rules and glorious nature of drinking games is to play them, in your own way, and provide yourself with your own set of happy memories.

Cocktail Recipes

Here are some favourite student cocktail recipes for those of you with a hint of class.

Piña Colada

Serves 1

- ◆ 1 shot white rum
- ◆ 2 shots coconut milk
- ◆ 2 shots pineapple juice

To decorate: strawberry and pineapple slices

Margarita

Serves 1

- ◆ 1.5 shots tequila
- ◆ 1 shot Cointreau
- ◆ 1-2 tablespoons fresh lime juice
- ◆ cracked ice

Tequila Sunrise

Serves 1

- ◆ 1 shot tequila

- ◆ 2 teaspoons grenadine
- ◆ 2.5 shots orange juice
- ◆ fruit slices to decorate

Bloody Mary

Serves 1

- ◆ 1 shot vodka
- ◆ 2 shots tomato juice
- ◆ squeeze of orange juice
- ◆ splash of Worcester sauce

Screwdriver

Serves 1

- ◆ 1 shot vodka
- ◆ juice of 1 orange
- ◆ ice cubes

Sangria

Serves 5+

- ◆ 2 bottles red wine
- ◆ 0.5 pint soda water
- ◆ 0.5 pint brandy (optional)
- ◆ ice cubes
- ◆ slices of fruit to decorate

Hawaiian Punch

(This recipe originated from the infamous windsurfing punch parties we went to, where you pay £3 for as much punch as you can drink).

Serves 4 +

- ◆ 1 bottle red wine
- ◆ 1 small bottle vodka
- ◆ 2 cartons orange juice
- ◆ 1 bottle lemonade
- ◆ 1 carton pineapple juice
- ◆ 4 shots Archers

Pulling Tips

A substantial proportion of your well-spent socialising time is likely to be pre-occupied by a phenomenon known as "pulling". University is a time of getting to know people – and some more intimately than others.

Tried & tested pulling tips and mistakes

◆ "Check their age. Also make sure they're not male – an adams apple is sometimes the only real way of telling." – **Tom Freemantle,** *2nd year Computer science*

◆ "Find an excuse to touch their body in some way, perhaps an affectionate punch or complimenting their clothes by touching them." – **Lisa Kirby,** *3rd year Biology*

◆ "Go out in drag – I find it helps"– **Neil Stewart,** *2nd year Law*

◆ "Don't get too pissed – even if you manage to attract the lucky lady, your performance in the bedroom won't stand up to much – literally." – **Steve Honeywell,** *2nd year Journalism*

◆ "Wear easy access clothing – I recommend Velcro". **Rina Patel,** *2nd year Medicine*

◆ "Check yourself out in the mirror before you approach them. Stray bogies and panda eyes might not go down well." **Maria Allen,** *1st year History of Art*

◆ "Let's face it, the only true way of winning a girl is by getting her pissed." – **Andrew Campbell,** *4th year Medicine*

DIARY OF A STUDENT

Alcohol can take its toll and humiliate you at any time or any place, as a school-friend of mine once experienced. Accompanied by his unruly mates they went to watch the Pilkington Cup Final at Twickenham, which was invariably played between Bath and Leicester (and invariably won by Bath – ah those were the days). In spite of his heroic morning drinking, he did manage to get into the stadium, and took his seat in the front row of the second tier of the ground. However, before the match even kicked off he projectile vomited onto the unsuspecting journalists and their laptops, in the press box below. Strangely enough this didn't go unnoticed, and he was promptly escorted from the stadium, more to protect him from the decorated reporters than anything else.

Moral of the story – while you may be able to get away with such misbehaviours as projectile vomiting over drunkard student mates whilst watching the game on the box, such actions will not be tolerated in the real world – try and restrict any serious drinking binges and their consequences to the confines of student life.

James Cox, *1st Year Computing and Mathematics*

CHAPTER

4

HEALTH AND WELFARE

Now that you're living away from home it is crucial to take responsibility for your own health. Although the university lifestyle encourages you to slip into a few bad habits, it is important to maintain a healthy lifestyle by eating, sleeping and exercising properly.

Freshers' Flu and Colds

University is a haven for colds and flu as your immune system can struggle to cope with late nights, alcohol binges and poor eating habits. Freshers' Week is renowned for the spreading of germs as a result of all the 'close contact' between new faces.

Most of us suffer from at least two colds a year, and whilst there is no cure for them there are ways to avoid and relieve the symptoms.

Tips:
- Drink plenty of fluids as it helps cleanse your system and stops your throat from becoming dry.
- Dose up on vitamin C as it helps to boost your immune system. Echinacea and zinc are also well known for building immunity.
- Keep yourself warm and try to get plenty of sleep.
- Ask at the chemist for any remedies that may temporarily relieve the symptoms. Medicines like Lemsips are useful for helping you carry on as normal.

The flu is often confused with heavy colds. You generally experience extra symptoms that you don't get with a cold which include high fevers, headaches, aching limbs, lack of energy and a 'shivery' feeling. Medicines aren't much use and even antibiotics won't help as flu is a virus, so again all you can do is follow the above advice.

"I think on average I got about 3 hours sleep a night during my first 2 weeks at uni, so I was hardly surprised that I caught the bug."

Meningitis

Meningitis, for all the attention in the Press, is a pretty rare disease but it is life threatening and needs urgent treatment. The bacteria which cause it are usually only spread in close contact situations, such as living together, kissing etc. Outbreaks are more likely to occur in places where people live or work closely together – so university halls are a prime target. Some (but not all) of the more serious types of meningitis can now be prevented by immunisation. Check that you have had your meningitis immunisation and, if not, talk to your surgery practice nurse. The important thing to know is that the disease develops very rapidly, usually within a matter of hours. The symptoms are not always easy to spot at first as they are initially similar to those you get with flu and can start with a simple sore throat and fever, but with meningitis things then rapidly get worse and the following symptoms develop:

◆ headache
◆ vomiting
◆ stiffness in the neck
◆ sensitivity to light

◆ fever
◆ rash which starts as tiny red pinpricks and develops into purple blood blisters. Do the 'glass test' to check: put a glass over the rash and apply pressure, if the spots don't "blanche", i.e. disappear, under the pressure, it could be a meningitis rash. But, be aware that only 40% of people with meningitis get the rash, so if you have the other symptoms listed above seek *urgent* medical attention. Early diagnosis could save your life.

ALCOHOL

The recommendations are that men should drink no more than 3-4 units a day and women 2-3 units a day.

One unit is equal to:
◆ 1 half pint of normal strength beer/lager.
◆ 1 small glass of wine.
◆ 1 pub measure spirits.
◆ 1 pub measure fortified wine e.g. sherry, martini.

For the average male this works out as 12 pints a week. This becomes a bit of a problem for university students when the average weekly recommendation is exceeded in a single Friday night at 'Pound a Pint'.

Drinking 'sensibly':

- ◆ Make sure you eat a good meal before you go out. If you are in a rush, drink a glass of milk as it helps to line your stomach.
- ◆ Try to pace yourself, as drinking quickly can suddenly hit you and you may find yourself out of control without even realising it.
- ◆ The dodgy kebab on the way home may not seem like the best idea the morning after, but food does help to absorb alcohol and lessen your hangover – unless of course you get food poisoning!
- ◆ Alternate alcoholic drinks with water and try and properly re-hydrate at the end of the night. Dehydration intensifies hangovers, so by drinking lots of water you can reduce your headache the next morning.
- ◆ Don't mix alcohol with other drugs as it can exaggerate their effect and have unpredicatable consequences.

The consequences of drinking

Hangovers - the blistering headache, the raw feeling in the stomach, the nausea and the difficulty trying to concentrate on even the smallest tasks would be enough to stop any sane person ever drinking again …..

Short-term risks – get plastered and have a good time but do remember that inebriates have a tendency to attract accidents – getting pregnant or falling downstairs and maiming yourself or vomiting in your sleep and maybe not waking up might not be quite the fun night you had in mind.

Long-term risks – apart from the risks of alcohol dependence and liver disease, regular heavy alcohol intake damages sexual potency, sporting performance and can aggravate depression. Bearing in mind we lose millions of brain cells every time we have a serious binge, it makes you wonder just how bright we would have been with that extra quadrillion brain cells that the average student loses at uni.

DRUGS

Depending on who you socialise with and where you go out, you will probably come into contact with drugs. The student environment provides opportunities to use or experiment with drugs if you choose to. Aside from being illegal, you should always bear in mind that taking any drug is a risk to both your physical and mental health. Do not encourage other people to take them against their will, and if you are the one being pressured you always have the power to say 'No'.

CONTRACEPTION

It is well known that students' pants are a hive of activity, and by 'nipping back for a quick coffee' it may be more than the caffeine keeping you up all night. But bear in mind that, while uni is a great excuse to have fun broadening your experiences, the fun carries with it a number of consequences. As well as the risk of pregnancy, there are a variety of infections that can be passed on through sex and therefore it is vital to act safely and take precautions during intercourse.

"Waiting for my period was an absolute nightmare. I couldn't sleep or concentrate on anything. I was convinced I was pregnant, and swore that I'd never have unprotected sex again."

Condoms

Condoms are the best way of protecting against sexually transmitted diseases (STDs). They are readily available in chemists, supermarkets and vending machines found in pub and club toilets. You can get them free from family planning clinics, sexual health clinics and Brook Advisory Centres.

Spermicides provide additional protection against pregnancy when used with a condom. You can buy it in foams, creams, pessaries and gels.

Women can also wear condoms. These fit inside the vagina and are available from most chemists.

Other methods of contraception do not protect you from sexually transmitted diseases but, on the other hand, barrier methods alone do not provide really cast iron protection against unwanted pregnancy. It may be sensible to use something like the Pill and a barrier with a new or unfamiliar partner. Get advice from your doctor or from the local Family Planning Clinic.

The Pill

The Pill is approximately 99.5% effective at protecting against pregnancy, *provided you take it correctly*. The Pill is available by prescription. There are a number of different types of Pill and your doctor will advise you as to which is most suitable for you.

Diaphragm/Cap

The diaphragm is inserted into the vagina before intercourse. It must be used with a spermicide and left in for 6 hours after sex. If used correctly it is 92–96% effective. It must be correctly sized and prescribed by a doctor or nurse.

Contraceptive injection

The contraceptive injection prevents ovulation for 12 weeks. It is at least 98% effective. One disadvantage is that any adverse side effects may last throughout the 12 week period. It's a good alternative for some people who can't take the Pill or can't remember to take the Pill regularly.

The Coil

Coils provide protection for up to 5 years at a time, but they won't be suitable for the majority of students because they are more aimed at women who have already had pregnancies.

EMERGENCY CONTRACEPTION

Morning-After Pill

These can be taken up to 72 hours (3 days) after sex. However, the sooner you take them after sex the better. They are available free from a doctor, family planning clinic, sexual health clinic or young persons clinic. You can also buy them from chemists for around £20. The morning after Pill is not as effective as using proper contraception.   Don't rely on it – get some proper regular contraception sorted.

IUD

Where there is a high risk of unwanted pregnancy and it is too late for the morning after Pill (i.e. over 72 hours after sex), a coil can be inserted by a family planning doctor which may prevent pregnancy for up to 5 days after sex. It is not a good or easy option and is something of a last resort.

Remember – neither form of emergency contraception will protect you from STDs – condoms are the most effective protection against these.

Sexually Transmitted Diseases

In most cases, neither you nor your partner will be aware of any STD. The safe bet is to use barrier contraception for all sex, except perhaps with a single long-term partner. Some types of STDs can cause permanent damage and infertility if left untreated. Therefore it is important to visit the doctor and receive treatment as soon as possible. If you think you may have an infection, visit your GP or GUM clinic (you can obtain information on these by calling the Family Planning Clinic helpline listed at the end of the chapter). GUM centres run drop-in clinics which you can turn up to without a pre-booked appointment and are completely confidential.

HIV & AIDS

AIDS (Acquired Immune Deficiency Syndrome) is a condition caused by a virus called HIV (Human Immunodeficiency Virus). This reduces the body's ability to defend itself against infection and eventually results in death.

HIV is spread through sexual intercourse (anal or vaginal) or by infected blood entering the bloodstream, for example through the sharing of needles. It cannot be spread by touching or drinking from the same cup. There is presently no cure for AIDS. You may not always know the full sexual history of each new partner and consequently it is vital that you practise safe sex.

HEPATITIS B & C

This can be spread through sexual contact and contact with bodily fluids such as blood, saliva and urine. The most important transmission is needle-sharing by drug-users. It can cause severe liver damage in some people.

CHLAMYDIA

If left untreated, chlamydia can cause a serious infection in women known as Pelvic Inflammatory Disease, which can cause infertility. Symptoms include:

◆ abnormal discharge from the vagina, urethra, penis or anus
◆ inflammation around the genital area
◆ pelvic pain during intercourse.

GONORRHOEA

Symptoms in men:

◆ burning pain on passing urine
◆ discharge from the penis
◆ irritation and discharge from the anus.

Most women do not experience any symptoms at all.

Gonorrhoea can be treated with antibiotics.

If you have any of the above symptoms of Chlamydia or Gonorrhoea you should seek advice from your GP or GUM clinic as soon as possible.

GENITAL WARTS

These are growths/warts of varying sizes on the genitals. They may develop up to a year after infection. They can be treated by application of an ointment.

Although harmless in men and cause no discomfort, they are now thought to be the main cause of abnormal cervical smears in the long term, so it is important not to pass them on by getting them treated.

GENITAL HERPES

These are characterised by small painful blisters on or around the genital area. They can be associated with flu-like symptoms such as headache, temperature and backache and a burning pain when passing urine. This is an unpleasant and recurring problem so it is irresponsible to have unprotected sex and pass it on to your partner if you think you may have it.

PUBIC LICE/CRABS

These are small lice that live in pubic hair. They can be spread by close body contact, sharing towels and bed linen and through sex. They can be treated by special lotions available from the pharmacist.

THRUSH

Thrush is not a sexually transmitted disease. Thrush is caused when naturally occurring yeasts multiply. Symptoms in women include a white vaginal discharge, itching, pain when passing urine and swelling of the vulva. Men may occasionally notice inflammation of the penis. It is easy to treat via your doctor or with over the counter treatment from the pharmacy.

CYSTITIS

Cystitis is also not an STD. It is caused by inflammation of the bladder. It causes burning when passing urine, and there is a need to urinate more frequently. It may help to drink lots of water, preferably mixed with bicarbonate of soda throughout the day. It is thought that drinking cranberry juice may also help. If the condition persists for more than 24 hours you should contact your doctor for advice.

"I felt really embarrassed having to go to the family planning clinic. But they were really nice, everything was done confidentially and it was such a relief to get the problem sorted out."

Eating Disorders

It is easy for girls (and sometimes boys) to become preoccupied with their weight and eating habits, especially when living away from home for the first time. Regular exercise and sensible eating are the best ways of controlling weight as oppose to strict dieting. Starvation is detrimental to your health and does not help you to lose weight in the long term as your metabolism decreases, meaning you use energy less efficiently.

It is not unusual to worry about your weight and feel guilty after a binge. However, if you:
◆ spend most of your time thinking about food,
◆ your weight fluctuates due to bingeing and starving, or
◆ you are making yourself sick after eating
then you should speak to a doctor and get help.

Stress

Although stress is a part of everyday life, there are periods such as exam time when we feel like we can no longer cope, and even simple things get on top of us.

Tell tale signs of stress:

- ◆ Do you lie awake worrying about the next day?
- ◆ Do you feel guilty when relaxing?
- ◆ Does life seem full of crises?
- ◆ Are you tense and impatient?
- ◆ Do you experience a dry mouth, sweaty palms or a thumping heart for no good reason?

If you have said 'yes' to any of these there is no need to panic as there are many ways to get your stress responses back in tune.

Ways to control stress:

- ◆ Try and increase your physical activity. Sport is an ideal way of relieving tension caused by stress, and will also encourage better sleep.
- ◆ If you are feeling stressed, take a deep breath and exhale slowly. A simple technique you could try is 'in with the good, out with the bad' – think of a good thing, such as a holiday or a friend and 'breathe' it in, then think of a bad thing, such as the person or thing making you stressed, and 'breathe' it out.
- ◆ Have proper breaks from whatever makes you feel stressed, and eat more slowly.
- ◆ Try meditation or yoga. Try stretching your arms or neck and smiling even if you don't feel like it – it does help.
- ◆ Avoid caffeine as it increases stress symptoms. Don't drink too much alcohol – it has a rebound anxiety effect.

PERSONAL SAFETY

One of the most important things is to let your flatmates or friends know your plans. Tell them where you are going and if you'll be staying out over night so they will know whether to expect you back.

If you are walking alone:

♦ Stick to well-lit routes.

♦ Avoid shortcuts through alleys or parks.

♦ Walk confidently and briskly.

♦ Do not stop to give the time or directions.

♦ Carry a mobile phone and a personal emergency alarm. The alarm is an instant deterrent, whereas a phone is useful to get help but it is not immediate enough. (Most Student Unions provide free or very cheap rape alarms for female students.)

"I decided I couldn't be bothered to wait for everyone to leave the pub, so I set off by myself. Five minutes away from my house I realised I was being followed. Although nothing happened, it really shook me up and I decided I'd never walk home alone again at night."

Transport

Taxis:
◆ Only use reputable taxi firms. Some towns now have minicabs driven by women for women.

Rail/Tube:
◆ Avoid empty carriages.
◆ Sit near other female passengers.

Cars:
◆ Lock the doors when driving.
◆ Park in well-lit areas in case you have to return to your car after dark.

In the home:
◆ Don't let strangers know your address, or that you'll be home alone.
◆ Have a chain on your front door so you can check who is there.
◆ Know your rights about Landlord entry etc.

Watch out for others:
◆ Walk a female back to her accommodation if she asks, or put her in a licensed minicab.
◆ Don't walk behind a person on their own as they may feel vulnerable. Similarly, a group of students together may appear threatening.
◆ Try to cross the road if someone is walking towards you on their own at night.

Date-Rape Drug

The 'date rape drug' is becoming more common across the UK. It is a dissolving tablet that can be slipped into your drink and cause temporary memory loss and confusion, allowing the victim to be taken advantage of, and in some cases - raped. To avoid the chance of this happening, don't let strangers buy your drinks, and never leave your glass unattended as someone could slip a tablet in.

Advice on Disabilities

Universities cater for students with a variety of disabilities; contact your university in advance to find out what help they have available. There is also a Disabled Students Allowance to help with the extra costs you may have as a direct result of your disability, and you do not have to repay this help.

Dyslexia

If you are dyslexic you can also receive financial help to put towards equipment such as computer programmes or dictaphones that may aid your learning. You may also be entitled to free extra tuition. Your

LEA will need evidence of your dyslexia from a qualified psychologist before they can decide which help is available for you.

Helplines and Contact Numbers

AIDS/HIV National Aids Helpline	0800 567123
DRINKLINE	0345 320202
DRUGS National Helpline	0800 776600
DYSLEXIA	
British Dyslexia Association's Helpline	0118 9668271
EATING DISORDERS	
Eating Disorders Helpline	01603621414
EMERGENCY CONTRACEPTION	
Emergency Contraception Helpline	0800 494847
FAMILY PLANNING CLINIC	02078 374044
MENINGITIS Meningitis Trust Helpline	0345 538118

DIARY OF A STUDENT

Last year in halls my flatmates ranked pretty low on the general health scale – besides the usual freshers flu, we had numerous plagues of boils, rashes, food poisoning, glandular fever and a pregnancy. But as the daughter of an ex-greengrocer, I bought and ate fruit and veg in bulk, so albeit the odd hangover, my vitamin supply kept me healthy and fuelled my rejection from the medical research companies who prey on students' ill-health, offering cash rewards for snot and acne samples. Yet once after celebrating the beginning of exams with a few drinks (clearly commemorating anything with alcohol), I prized open a tin of sweetcorn and my thumb in the process. My well-prepared, slightly inebriated flatmates bandaged my hand up so tight it turned blue, rushed me to hospital and arranged shifts to stay with me in-between their revision timetables, and whilst it wasn't my writing hand I cut, my department were also great and took my injury into consideration when marking my exams. The moral of this story should be 'be careful when drinking and using appliances as a serious accidents may occur'. However, everyone was so helpful in dressing, cooking, washing up and making allowances for me that I began to enjoy it...unfortunately a year later my new flatmates are unconvinced by my feigned relapses from acute thumb disorder and my lecturers are no longer still buying the excuse.

Jessica Rees, *2nd Year, English Literature*

CHAPTER 5

MONEY

Learning to cope financially for the first time away from home may prove to be a bit of a nightmare for some students. When the bills are overdue, the bank refuses to give you any more money, you're up to your ears in debt and your remaining food ingredients consist of ketchup and spaghetti hoops - there may be reason to panic. However, by organising your money sensibly you can avoid such financial worries and will be able to live a lot more cheaply than you think.

Investing In A Degree

For some, the decision of whether to go to university may boil down to a question of money. The Barclays Graduate Survey 2000 found that 85% of students interviewed were currently in debt. The average graduate debt level is presently estimated at £10,000.

Faced with figures such as these it is hardly surprising that students are put off from going to university. However, you should remember that the long-term benefits of a degree usually outweigh the short-term problems of debt. Think of your degree as an investment in the future - a passport to the job you want.

Studies show that:
◆ the long-term incomes of graduates are higher than those without a degree.
◆ 47% of graduates are in permanent employment in their preferred career within 6 months of leaving uni.
◆ the average salary upon leaving has risen to £15,000. Furthermore, with a degree your income is likely to rise more rapidly.
◆ the chances of becoming unemployed are reduced by 50%.

The Cost of Being a Student

Tuition fees

Tuition fees cost up to £1,075 in 2001/02. The rest of the cost of the course (on average £4000), is automatically paid for you. The amount you pay annually for your tuition fees depends upon the income of your parents.

Residual Family Income	Tuition Fees
£29,784 and above	Pay full £1,075
Between £20,000 - £29,784	Pay part fees
Less than £20,000	Don't pay fees

Students must complete a form providing details of their family financial circumstances, which the local education authority (LEA) uses to calculate the exact fees payable. If your gross family income exceeds £29,784 you will be expected to pay the full £1,075.

The annual cost of living

Below is a rough guide to costs of student life. Naturally, this will vary according to your location, course, stomach size and how much of a lightweight you are.

Average expenditure per annum

	inside London	outside London
Tuition fees	£1,075	£1,075
Books/equipment etc.	£251	£251
Photocopying	£82	£82
Rent	£2,396	£1,683
Fuel	£384	£384
Food/household goods	£1,266	£1,064
Laundry	£102	£102
Insurance	£96	£54
Clothing	£410	£410
Travel	£696	£444
Leisure (going out)	£953	£794
TOTAL	**£7,711**	**£6,348**

Loans

For many, university would be impossible without the aid of a loan. The size of loan awarded to you depends on a number of factors including your income and that of your parents and whether or not you will be studying in London. Your local education authority has the final decision on the amount of loan you are entitled to. It is then up to you to decide how much of this you wish to borrow. You will receive this amount in 3 instalments at the start of each semester.

What are students entitled to?

Maximum student loan available in 2001/2002

	Full Year	Final Year Students
Studying in London	£4,700	£4,075
Studying outside of London	£3,815	£3,310
At parental home	£3,020	£2,635

"Before I went to uni I found it a daunting thought knowing I would be living on borrowed money, but it was the only way that I could fund going. However, when I got there I realised virtually everyone has to do the same, and it was reassuring to know I wasn't the only one going to be in debt when I left."

Repayment

Unfortunately loans are just that – a loan – and eventually you will have to start repaying them, usually starting the April after you have graduated (or left the course). The amount you have to repay depends on your income and there is no set period within which the loan must be repaid. The rate of repayment is 9% of income each year when you are earning over £10,000. You do not have to make repayments while your income is below £10,000.

Hardship loans

If you do have problems paying your fees you should contact your student union or financial support centre as there are hardship loans available for those students that need extra help. It is up to your university to decide whether you meet their criteria for a hardship loan and how much you can receive. The loans are available in amounts of £100 up to £500.

JOBS

Part-time jobs

Paid employment during term-times and holidays can make a huge difference to the extent of debt you will be faced with upon leaving uni. You should consider your options early on in the university year. One of the best places to try is in the university itself - in the bar, shop or sports centre.

"I worked in our union bar, and whilst the pay wasn't amazing, it was very sociable as we were all students and used to go out together after work, or even stay back at the bar and have some drinks."

Finding work in a big city is unlikely to be a problem as there will inevitably be a range of jobs available in pubs, clubs, shops and restaurants. Your university may have a notice-board or a job-shop showing what's on offer and it may also be worth inquiring at your local job centre. If you join a part-time work agency the staff will call you with any work that is available and it is up to you if you choose to take it; the positives are that the pay is usually good and the hours are flexible.

While term-time employment is a necessity for many, it is important not to let it interfere with your degree. Some students end up working so many hours a week that they sacrifice studying time. While a part-time job may justify the extra night's drinking, a degree will affect your future employability and there is potentially a lot more at stake. It is vital to get the balance right.

Summer jobs

Whatever work you manage to get in the summer will help to cut the debt. Skills such as punctuality, good communication skills and the ability to build good working relationships will look good on your CV, whether you gained them working at MacDonalds or for a large law firm.

By pursuing a summer job connected with your career aims, you can gain a greater understanding of the workplace and get an idea of whether you really are interested in that line of work. It can equip you with useful transferable skills that will impress future employers. Businesses often take on undergraduates each summer for up to 3 months. It is worth writing off for an application form well in advance, as there may be substantial competition. If you impress the company sufficiently they may even offer you a future job.

Summer jobs abroad

Working abroad is a great way to broaden your experience of different countries, without adding to your debt. It is also a chance to meet new people and develop your independence in unfamiliar surroundings. Whether it's working on a kibbutz in Israel, a café in Spain or au-pairing in the USA, organising such a job requires pre-planning, research and guts. Any contacts you have may come in handy, otherwise you might wish to join up with a charitable or commercial organisation who will assist you in arranging the work.

"I worked in Spain for 3 months teaching English. I had an amazing summer, met loads of new people, paid off my overdraft and as an added bonus got a wicked suntan!"

Organisations such as BUNAC and Camp America arrange for students to work and travel in the USA. They arrange accommodation, travel and work, and students pay for flights and a nominal administration fee. They provide a rare opportunity to work in places that it would normally be difficult to get a working visa for.

Sponsorship

Sponsorship through a company is an ideal way of easing financial pressures at uni. A company may pay your tuition fees, or even living costs, and in return you may be contracted to work for that company after graduation.

More and more universities and charitable organisations are providing scholarships, bursaries and grants and you should check your university prospectus to find out about these. Ordinarily you should think about applying for these when you complete your UCAS form, however, a number of companies only offer sponsorship to students who are already at university.

Bank Accounts

Banks are, believe it or not, geared to help you through your financial worries at university. It is important that you chose your bank carefully, as you may need to deal with them a lot during your student years and beyond.

Tips on choosing a bank

◆ Don't be overly influenced by any freebies offered when you open an account. Long-term you will benefit much more from a bank who will give you the best deals on overdrafts and loans than you will from a free CD voucher.

◆ Choose a bank that has plenty of cash machines and a convenient local branch. You are likely to need to contact them fairly often.

◆ Talk to other students who have accounts in different banks and find out what their experience has been before you make your choice.

◆ Questions to ask:

 - What is the rate of interest?
 - Will I get a free overdraft facility and if so how much?
 - How easily can I extend my overdraft and what will be the rate of interest on this?
 - How much interest will I be charged for unauthorised overdrafts?
 - How long do I have to pay off any debts after leaving university?

"I waited until I arrived at university before I opened a student account, but as it turned out, everyone had the same idea. The queues were huge and I had already had enough of this in enrolment, so my 3-hour wait at the bank was not very welcome. Try and organise a bank account before you arrive as it will save time and mean you have a secure account to pay your loan cheques into immediately."

What the banks offer

Big banks such as Barclays and NatWest offer many incentives to students to open up accounts with them. These are some of the current offers available:

Lloyds

- Interest-free overdraft up to £1500.
- £40 cash.
- Current account debit card.
- Free banking.
- Commission free foreign currency.
- Internet and telephone banking.
- An Asset credit card, on application.

Barclays

- Maximum overdraft of £3000.
- Up to £1,250 of that overdraft interest-free.
- 15% off vouchers for books, CDs and videos at Waterstones and HMV.
- A £30 book, CD or video voucher.
- Student Barclaycard with no annual fee.
- Barclays Connect debit card.
- Free online banking.
- Instant Savings Account with free automatic transfer.
- Commission-free travel money.

NatWest

- Telephone and internet banking.
- Interest-free overdraft.
- Fee-free Natwest Student Mastercard.
- 24-hour banking.
- CD vouchers.
- Natwest Servicecard.

HSBC

- Interest-free overdraft up to:
    - 1st year: £750
    - 2nd year: £1,000
    - 3rd year: £1,250
    - subsequent years: £1,500.
- No overdraft fees.
- Either £50 cash or a 4-year Young-person's Railcard.
- Fee-free Mastercard credit card with £500 limit.
- £100 International Debit Card and cheque-book.
- Student counsellor service.
- 24-hour telephone banking service.
- Automatic transfer to 3-year graduate service.

Money Saving Tips

You'll be surprised at how by following a few pieces of simple advice, you can work miracles in stretching your pennies to make ends meet and reduce the mountain of debt characteristic of student life.

◆ Learn to budget sensibly

Draw up a budget and stick to it. Start by working out your total income, including loans, part-time work, parental contributions and any personal savings and how long you have to make it last. Subtract any costs which must be paid up-front and then list all likely expenditures including bills, accommodation fees, going out, food and travel expenses which must then be deducted from the total money coming in.

◆ Put loan money into a savings account

Even if you don't need a loan when you start at uni, it might be worth applying for one anyway and putting it into a savings account to earn interest. Then if you need it you can use it at a later stage.

◆ Don't open more than one bank account

If you do this, you may find that you end up with two overdrafts. This may seem like a good idea at the time, but it is potentially bad news in the long run when you have to start thinking about repayments.

◆ Steer clear of credit cards

Avoid store cards or credit cards with high monthly repayments. It makes it difficult to keep track of outgoing expenditures and if you don't manage to pay bills on time the interest payable may add up. It could become a very expensive way of spending.

◆ Don't buy every book on your reading list

Talk to tutors and students who have taken the course to find out which books are most important. Some books may be available in the library. If you can, buy second-hand books or share them with friends.

◆ Don't feast on gourmet food

Look for special offers and bargains at supermarkets. Try and go late in the evening when many fresh foods are reduced, or shop at market stalls. Buy supermarket own brands (don't worry, you'll soon be used to economy foods and forget you ever used to eat luxuries such as Heinz). Buy food in bulk and share with housemates and learn some cheap recipe ideas (see recipe section).

◆ Take lunch with you

If you are out for the day, take lunch with you and re-fill water bottles to save buying a new one everyday. It may seem like a hassle when you're in a rush in the morning but it's amazing how much you will save in a week by not buying lunch out.

◆ Make the most of your NUS discount

Many leisure activities offer discounts for students, by showing your NUS card you can often get reduced rates in clothes shops, cinemas, restaurants, swimming pools etc.

◆ Avoid expensive clothes shopping

Shop around at second-hand clothes shops or ask for more expensive items as birthday or Christmas presents.

"Whenever I go charity shopping the only clothes I seem to find are old men's brown smelly dungarees, but many people assure me there are bargains to be found."

especially

◆ Seek out student nights and union entertainment

Prices at university bars and clubs are usually much cheaper than those in town, especially at weekends, so they may be the better budget option for nights out. If you have a habit of going out and losing any inhibitions of whacking up £50 on your credit card, leave your credit cards and cheque-book behind. Set yourself a spending limit. Drinking at home or at friends' houses before you go out is a sociable way of saving money.

"Offer to buy the last round of the night – then everyone's too pissed to know you haven't bought it."

◆ Keep transport costs to a minimum

Walk or cycle wherever possible to avoid daily fares. Student rail and coach cards can save considerable money on long-distance journeys so may be a worthwhile investment if you travel a lot.

◆ Buy a phone-card

Although most of us have mobiles, a phone-card or charge-card may be a cheaper way of making long calls.

DIARY OF A STUDENT

My first term at uni was amazing; I went out virtually every night – to the union, to clubs, pub crawls – at the very least it would be a few pints at the campus bar. I had no reservations about money as I bought round after round. A couple of weeks before the end of the first semester I realised that I was up to my overdraft limit, and all I had to show for it was the dark rings under my eyes. This came as a bit of a shock: my liver started to dry up, I began eating economy pasta morning, noon and night and I became known as the lame-ass that stayed in on Friday nights when everyone headed off to the pub. I even made the odd 9.00am lecture. I think the most depressing thing was watching my friends get ready for the ball, starting drinking at 3 in the afternoon when I didn't have a hope in hell of raising the money to afford it. It seemed like an eternity until the next loan came in. I certainly learnt my lesson, the next term I sorted out a job in a bar two evenings a week and limited my nights out to 3 a week. Having experienced the trauma of living life at uni on no cash, I will make damn sure I never have to do it again!

John Morris, *3rd Year Biochemistry*

CHAPTER 6

GETTING A HOUSE

The majority of students choose to live in halls during their first year of university and then move into a house for their second and third years. There are various advantages and disadvantages of both.

HALLS OF RESIDENCE OR A HOUSE?

The advantages and disadvantages of halls

Advantages

- Being so close to many other students makes it potentially easier to make friends.
- Many facilities are often close at hand, such as sports amenities, shop, bar and laundry.
- Accommodation fees usually cover bills which saves much hassle and may work out less expensive.
- Repairs can normally be sorted out straightforwardly by reporting them to the campus office.
- If in catered halls, you don't have to worry about cooking and might be more inclined to eat properly.
- Campuses are usually much safer than city streets as there are lots of other people in close proximity. They are usually well-lit and many universities have wardens and camera security.
- If you're really lucky you might get a cleaner to clean your kitchen – although in our case this came hand-in-hand with £5 fines for not changing bin-bags etc.

Disadvantages

- Rooms can be small and impersonal and might not feel homely. You may not be allowed to decorate them as you want to.
- Constant noise and distractions can become annoying, especially if you're in need of a good night's sleep when the flat downstairs decides to hold a party.
- Catered students may find that they don't like the food or don't want to eat at times meals are offered.

The advantages and disadvantages of houses

Advantages

- You can usually decorate your house as you wish and make it feel generally more home-like.
- You can choose the location of your house.
- You can choose who to live with.
- If you find a good house in your second year, you save the effort of moving house again in the third year.

Disadvantages

- Finding a house that you all like in an ideal location is rarely easy and you may have to trail around for several weeks before you succeed.
- You have to start being responsible for paying bills - a big hassle for even the most organised of people.

- ◆ Houses close to the university are often old and because they are relatively cheap can be of poor quality. They are therefore not renowned for their cleanliness and class. Green mouldy walls, rats and decaying furniture are not uncommon in student houses.
- ◆ You have to deal with landlords and housing agencies and co-operation is not always easy.
- ◆ You may become lonely if your flatmates aren't around, since you won't be so close to other students.

Don't rush into renting

If you do decide to rent a house the most important thing to remember is not to rush in. A lot of housing agencies and landlords advertise very early in the academic year which creates a snowballing panic amongst students who fear all the best houses will be snapped up. This is not the case as new houses are continually being advertised. You are unlikely to be left in the lurch. Also, you may have to pay full or half rent over the summer even though you won't be living there.

Choosing Your Housemates

Choosing who you are going to live with next year can be a stressful experience as people may already have a house arranged or there may be a group of you that's too big to all live together. Here are some points to bear in mind when choosing your housemates:

◆ Do you want to live in a mixed or single sex house?
◆ Would you prefer to live in a very sociable house or a quieter one?
◆ Do you all want to live in a similar location and pay a similar amount of rent?
◆ Do you want to live in a smoking or non-smoking house?
◆ Condider *not* living with people who are all on your course. It may prove too much living and working together.

- ◆ Try and live with someone with a car – (cheeky but very useful).
- ◆ The most important thing is to live with people who you think are reliable and that you can trust.

Try not to worry too much if you don't manage to live with your first choice of friends. Just remember, in your first year you were probably chucked in with a lot of strangers and things generally work out. Also, having some of your friends elsewhere gives you another house to seek refuge in if you need a break from your own.

If you find yourself without a group of housemates, put aside those thoughts of living in a bed-sit on your own as there are always notices around university where already established houses are looking for one or two new people to share with.

Choosing a House and Location

Although laws exist to ensure that rented houses are safe, unfortunately there are many irresponsible landlords, and students are among the most vulnerable tenants. Consequently finding a good house in a nice location is not always a smooth process, but by being aware of your rights you can keep hassles to a minimum. There are plenty of services and professionals who can give you advice and support throughout the whole process and you should make the most of any help available.

Agent or Landlord?

◆ Private Landlord

If possible, try and get a list of private landlords from your student union. These will either be properties which have been checked out by the university or have had to produce a Gas Safety Certificate in order to display property details. You could also try looking in your local paper. The advantage with using a private landlord is that you don't have to pay an agency fee.

◆ Agency-owned Properties

These properties are owned by the agency who acts as the landlord. You therefore pay rent and bond money to the agency.

◆ Agency-managed properties

In this case the landlord owns the house and the agency looks after it. You usually deal with the agency in reporting any problems and paying rent etc.

◆ Private Landlords found through an agency

This occurs when you find a property through an agency, and from then on you will deal with the landlord and rent etc. is paid directly to the landlord.

"We thought all agency fees were standard, so had no qualms about paying £150 each. It was gutting to find out we could have saved ourselves £50 by shopping around a bit."

The Contract

You will need to sign a contract with the agency/landlord outlining the rights and obligations of the tenant and landlord. It will state the length of tenancy, rent payable and how often it has to be paid.

You should read the contract thoroughly and understand its content. Once it has been signed you will not be able to break it without the agreement of the landlord or agency.

The Bond

You normally have to pay a deposit known as your "bond" which the agency retains throughout the year and will use to cover the costs of any cleaning or damage which has occurred during your stay.

"After living in the same house for two years, we were all quite proud that we hadn't broken or damaged anything, so were expecting to receive our bond back in full. What we didn't realise was that the general scum we left in kitchen for the new occupants to find was actually cleared up by a cleaner and the expense was deducted from our bond."

House Hunting Tips

◆ Choose a suitable location

Plan ahead by choosing a house close to the university, corner shop, supermarket, pub or whatever is important to you. If you live far away from the shops, carrying eight shopping bags back miles every week in the rain is a big hassle. Likewise, being a long way from your university building may put you off getting up for that 9.00am lecture, and you really don't need any other excuses. If possible, choose a house in a safe location on a well-lit road in case there is an instance when you have to walk home alone at night.

◆ Don't rush into anything
Don't rush into signing for a house. Your agency may try and rush you into choosing a house by suggesting that if you don't hurry the houses will be rented to someone else. In reality it is more likely that they are keen to get your agency fee into the bank and save manpower by not traipsing round any more houses with you. Admittedly, good houses in nice locations are unlikely to be on the market for long, but they come up all the time and by settling for a less than satisfactory house you might miss out on a better one that becomes available later.

◆ Split up
You can save time if you each approach 1 or 2 housing agencies and ask to be shown the best properties within your price range. When one of you thinks that you have found a suitable house, then you can all go back and have another look at a later date.

◆ Ask questions
Any decent agency should be happy to give you information on the property, so make sure you make the most of this and ensure you have explored all potential pitfalls before you sign anything.

◆ Find out about hidden costs and agency fees

Some houses may have unforeseen expenses on top of rent and you may find yourself paying more than you bargained for. For example, some properties have water meters rather than a flat water rate, which could potentially work out more costly. Ensure you are aware of what is included in the rent – paying more for better facilities may work out cheaper. Also check if the agency charges high fees for lease signings and inventories.

◆ Check that the property is safe

This should be your most important consideration in choosing a house. Ask to see a Gas Safety Certificate on every gas appliance. The best landlords will also provide fire extinguishers and smoke alarms. Furniture should preferably be British Standard-approved.

◆ Speak to current tenants

Try and speak to the previous tenants about any problems they encountered with the house or landlord, as this will give you a good indication as to how co-operative the landlord is likely to be.

"Two of the students who lived in the house we were looking at were there when we visited. We asked them why they were moving and they told us the house is freezing in winter and the traffic noise keeps them awake at night. It was worth asking as we didn't want to experience the same problems."

◆ Look for signs of damp

Condensation comes as standard in many student properties, but damp exists in varying degrees. Minor condensation is usually just the result of poor ventilation. If you are worried get someone who knows what they are looking for to check out the extent of the problem. If you decide to go ahead and take the risk anyway ask the landlord to provide better ventilation. Rising damp is a much more serious issue. Avoid signing for any property that you suspect may have rising damp. Green spotty walls are not the ideal way of decorating your house.

◆ Try and overlook furnishings that will be removed

A house that looks great when you initially look around it will more than likely be gutted of many of its contents when the existing tenants move out. The 1970s moth-eaten curtains will be hung back up and the rugs will be removed to reveal the stained fraying carpets ready for when you move in. Check how much of the decoration belongs to the tenants and how much comes with the house.

Choosing Rooms

In most houses you are looking at to rent there is generally one fantastic room and one death pit of a room and the others fall somewhere in between. Here are a selection of various tried and tested methods of how you can fairly go about choosing who gets which room.

The diplomatic sit round and 'discuss' it

This method usually fails abysmally as most people want to seem polite and flexible in front of their new housemates. They try and say, in the most roundabout way possible, that they want the biggest room. If there is one considerably smaller room than the others, you could all agree that whoever has it could pay slightly less rent.

Twister

Get an independent adjudicator to spin the arrow and oversee to make sure no cheating happens. Do it in rounds – whoever remains without falling onto the mat gets first choice of room. Then start round 2 for the second choice of rooms, again whoever remains without touching the mat has the next choice.

Dares

Whoever is prepared to go the furthest gets the best room. This one could get a bit messy as it is ideally played over a few drinks. The boys in our house had to order kebabs with their trousers round their ankles – (although we can't advise this one as it's indecent exposure and anyway, since then we've all been banned from eating there).

Names out of a hat

Tends to be the simplest way of choosing the rooms. The first person's name that comes out of the hat has first choice. The second name has second choice etc.

Dealing with Landlords

Student landlords or agencies generally receive a bad press, and whilst some may be sharks, try and be nice to your landlord or agent - it's in your best interest. Make an effort to tidy up before their visit as they are more likely to be co-operative if you are reasonable and show that you are prepared to look after the property as a responsible tenant.

What rights does the landlord have?

The landlord or their agent, has the legal right to enter the property at reasonable times of day to carry out the repairs for which they are responsible and to inspect the condition and state of repair of the property. They must give 24 hours' notice in writing of an inspection.

What rights does the tenant have?

The landlord cannot evict you without a possession order from the court. Matters such as whether you can keep animals etc. should be negotiated and included in the terms of the tenancy agreement.

Repairs

The landlord is usually responsible for repairs to:
◆ the structure and exterior of the property
◆ baths, sinks, showers etc
◆ heating and hot water installation.
The landlord is not responsible for repairing damage caused by you.

Inventory

When you first move into private rented accommodation you should be given a form to fill in called an inventory, which lists the contents of the property and the condition it's in. Be sure to fill this in properly as if you just tick all the boxes, such as one saying 'table provided' and one isn't, then at the end of your renting they will look back over the inventory and see that now it is missing and will be able to charge you for it.

ßILLS

This will probably be the first time in your life that you are confronted with the nightmare of bill-paying. You will receive regular water, gas, electricity and phone bills which you must pay by the deadline specified otherwise you may be cut off (in which case you must pay a reconnection fee), or threatened with legal action.

You may want to allocate the bills amongst housemates so that each person is responsible for paying one bill and collecting the divided amount of money from each of the other housemates.

Another idea is to open a joint account out of which bills are direct debited, and each housemate makes equal contributions to the account. The disadvantage with this is that you have to provide large sums of money upfront and people may not be able to afford it in one go.

For the phone bill, have a pad by the phone to write down all the numbers you have dialled, then make sure your phone bills are itemised so you can each add up your own calls. This is more difficult than it sounds though as mysterious numbers are frequently denied.

"We had a portable phone which I wouldn't recommend. It would always go missing so there was no way of keeping a pad by the phone to jot down who we'd each called. Sorting out the phone bill became a real problem."

Ways of minimising electricity bills

◆ Boiling the kettle uses a lot of energy so don't fill it to the top every time you just want one cup of tea.

◆ Use smaller hobs for smaller saucepans.

◆ Have showers more regularly than baths.

◆ Put on an extra jumper rather than turning up the heating.

◆ Set your heating on a timer so that it is not on constantly when you are out.

◆ Fit your windows with decent curtains and ask for any poor-fitting windows causing drafts to be repaired.

◆ Use the phone after peak time.

◆ Don't under-fill the washing machine or use it to wash one pair of socks (as one of our less economically-friendly housemates once did).

Insurance

It is a well-known fact that the vast majority of students leave their student houses empty during the holidays. They are generally not the securest of places, and consequently burglaries are quite common. The value of your possessions may add up to thousands of pounds so it is in your best interests to take out insurance.

Endsleigh Insurance is recommended by the National Union of Students as the best insurance company for students. From around £18 a year you can secure peace of mind that your possessions are covered. In the case of loss they will be replaced following a claim on a new for old basis, which means you receive new items at today's prices. The following cover options are available:

1. **Contents of your room** (between £2000 and £5000).
2. **Items that you take outside your room** (all risks) e.g. watches, jewellery, cameras etc.
3. **Computer equipment** (all risks) – covers accidental loss or damage.

Automatically included in this cover is legal liability, liability for loss or damage, personal injury, personal money from your room and cover during vacations. You can take out additional insurance for mobile phones.

It really is worth taking out insurance – coming back after a nice Christmas holiday to a ransacked house is disturbing enough without the additional worry that you are not covered.

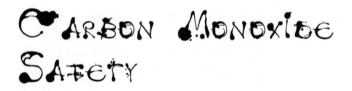

CARBON MONOXIDE SAFETY

Every year approximately 50 people die from carbon monoxide poisoning. Carbon monoxide can escape from appliances which have not been properly installed or maintained.

The danger of carbon monoxide is that you can't smell, see or taste it. It can kill in a matter of hours. Common symptoms of carbon monoxide poisoning are:

◆ Headaches
◆ Tiredness
◆ Dizziness
◆ Chest and stomach pains
◆ Sickness.

Safety checks

Look out for signs of staining, soot or discolouration around gas appliances such as boilers, fires and water heaters and yellow or red flames from pilot lights.

Never cover an appliance or block its ventilation.

If you have any worries you should turn off the appliance, open the windows and contact the gas board as soon as possible.

Handy House Tips

Keeping your house tidy

As petty as it sounds, the issue of cleaning is the main cause of arguments in student houses. Most houses have their own rules or rotas, but here's what worked for us:

Washing up. We came up with the idea of having separate washing up bowls. We bought 5 different coloured washing up bowls for 50p each from a discount store, and placed them along our windowsill. It works well as if you don't have time to wash up you can put the stuff straight into your individual bowls and it stops the kitchen from being cluttered up by 3 week old crusty pasta pans.

Another common method of keeping on top of the washing up is having one person in charge of it per day. The downside of this is if that person has gone home then no-one wants to offer their services.

Cleaning. To keep the house clean we split it up into areas that we were each in charge of. This works well as you feel responsible for keeping your designated area tidy, and if you aren't doing it properly people know who to pin the blame on. Between the 5 of us this worked out as:-

- ◆ 2 people – kitchen (wipe surfaces and clean hob)
- ◆ 1 person – bathroom and hall (clean toilet and sink and hoover)
- ◆ 1 person – bin (empty daily and put bins out)
- ◆ 1 person – lounge (hoover and keep tidy)

Household goods kitty

At the start of each semester you could each put £10 into a kitty for things like toilet roll, washing up liquid, oven cleaner, bin liners, hoover bags etc.

"Next year we've decided to have a house kitty. I think the turning point was when I started using my shampoo as washing up liquid for the third week running as everyone was refusing to buy any new liquid and surprisingly we all seemed to have bought the last bottle."

Food sharing

Some houses like to share food, which is a nice communal gesture, but it doesn't always work out fairly. One of the easiest methods is to have a food kitty for the essentials, such as tea, coffee, milk, bread and butter, and buy other things separately.

Cheap ways of decorating

Contrary to popular belief, not all students live in squalor. Here are a few cost effective ways of making your house that bit more homely:

◆ **Paint** – brighten up a dull room entirely with a quick coat of paint.

◆ **Posters** – visit the poster sale and use them to cover up peeling wallpaper.

◆ **Throws** – a new sofa is probably out your price range, but throws are a cheap way of spicing up the look of a room and are also washable.

◆ **Plants** – give any student house a more homely look; try and find ones that need as little TLC as possible.

◆ **Lighting** – if your room seems a bit dark try using a higher watt light bulb, or if you want an atmospheric look use a painted light bulb to give a coloured glow to the room.

◆ **Curtains** – most houses come with pretty foul curtains but you can take then down and use bamboo blinds which are very cheap at £5 for a normal sized window.

◆ **Rugs** – if the carpets look about 40 years old and your landlord is refusing to change them, you can always buy a big rug to throw over the top.

◆ **Photos** – create a house photo board in a communal area. Photos add a personal touch to any room and embarrassing ones are a good talking point with visitors.

NB be careful how many changes you make to your house as you may lose your deposit. Check with your landlord before you do

DIARY OF A STUDENT

At the time I was supposed to be house hunting with my friends I saw a last minute holiday deal so zoomed off for a cheap bit of winter sun, leaving all the hassle of searching for a house in my friends' capable hands. My zero effort or concern for finding a place meant I didn't get a say in which room I had – and as a result got lumbered with the smallest one. There was just enough room for a bed, and my desk was the size of an A4 pad, which meant I had to keep all my stuff on the landing outside. That wasn't the worst part – within a week of living there we noticed droppings that looked suspiciously rat shaped (we are authorities on these issues), so spent the next few months in fear of finding a rat sharing our kitchen. My friends didn't notice the lack of double glazing when they visited the house on a warm day, but we spent most nights huddled round the TV each with 6 layers on. Other delights of living there included discovering mushrooms growing in our bathroom (honestly), and having a permanently blocked drain which meant you really wouldn't want to go into the garden.

Whether we liked it or not we were stuck there for a year, and whilst it wasn't quite the home I'd been used to it was certainly a learning experience. Next year I'll make sure I'm not on holiday on house hunting day.

Fliss Campbell, *2nd Year Leisure and Tourism*

CHAPTER 7

UNIVERSITY AND BEYOND

You'll be surprised at how quickly your time at university flies by, and before you realise it the world of interviews and responsibilities looms closer. So, what to do next? A large proportion of students will have completed their finals and still won't know which direction to go in. There is no need to panic as you have many options, so take a step back and assess the opportunities that are available.

#

Postgraduate study

An increasingly large number of finalists are choosing to continue their study. For some it's a chance to improve their career prospects and for others it's a way of putting off that leap into the harsh world of paid employment and remain as a care-free student.

Pros
◆ You have a chance to study at the highest level with some of the leading academics in the country in a subject that really interests you.
◆ It should substantially improve your employability.

Cons
◆ Postgraduate study is hard work and intensive.
◆ It is also expensive and you may have to take out another loan because outside funding is difficult to come by.

Year out/travelling

An appealing option is to go travelling or take a year out after you've finished the hard slog of finals.

Pros

- It may be the perfect chance to experience different cultures and places as once you have settled into a career you may not have the opportunity to take time off.
- It is a fantastic break after 3 years of lectures.

Cons

- The majority of students are in debt when they leave university, and it is likely you would incur further debts by travelling.
- Some employees may not see a year abroad as worthwhile, so try and do something positive if you go away. Unpaid volunteer work on your travels develops your skills base and shows you have a committed attitude. It may also equip your CV with a well-respected reference.

Career

You may decide you've had enough of always being skint and that you are ready to face life outside of university.

Pros

- You get a head start from your peers who are travelling or studying still.
- It is financially rewarding and you will be able to begin paying off your student loans.

Cons

◆ You may feel like your youth has suddenly ended as the alcoholic binges and rampant nights out have to be curbed for the 7.30am alarm that you'll be getting used to.

"I decided to go straight into a career and get earning, but I certainly got itchy feet when I was receiving e-mails from my friends who were in Sydney and Fiji and I was sat in an office."

Don't feel you are confined to only one of these choices, it is perfectly feasible to do all three, you could do further study, go travelling and then focus on your career - if you can organise it.

Job Hunting...

If you know what type of job you're looking for then great, however, if you're not sure ask yourself a few of these questions to decide what 'type' of job suits you.

Do you want…
◆ a job dealing with people?
◆ a job that allows you to travel?
◆ a routine nine to five job?
◆ a job that allows you to be creative?
◆ a job which gives you qualifications?
◆ a job with managerial prospects?

Work experience

A good way to discover the right career path is through work experience. It gives you hands-on experience in a variety of areas, allowing you to sample the different opportunities available. Experience in the work place is also increasingly valued by employers. You can do as little or as much as you like, from 4 hours to 4 months, and depending what field you are applying in - you can even be paid for your experience.

Where to look

There are many places you can begin looking for a job, don't just wait for one to come to you – get out there and search.

The Web. The internet has become an essential tool for finding work in recent years. A survey found that 89% of graduate recruiters advertised vacancies online.

National and Local Press. The national press tend to advertise jobs for different sectors of employment on specific days each week, whilst the local press is more suited for vacancies in smaller firms.

Specialist Press. The majority of occupations have their own specialist publications and journals with employment opportunities. These can be found in university or local libraries.

Graduate Vacancy bulletins. 'PROSPECTS For The Finalist' and 'PROSPECTS Today' are national graduation vacancy bulletins advertising forward and current vacancies respectively and are available from all HE Careers Services.

Recruitment Agencies. You may want to register with a specialist recruitment agency depending on what type of job you are after.

Graduate Fairs. They are designed for new graduates and there is a national fair held each Autumn in London and various universities hold their own fairs so ask at your Union or careers office.

Job Centres. These hold details on a wide range of vacancies, it is a free public service aimed at helping people find work.

Speculative Letters. Only half of all vacancies are advertised which means that many positions are filled through making enquires and writing speculative letters. If there is a company you would particularly like to work for there is no harm done by sending your CV. Even if there is no job available at the moment, your CV may be kept on file for any further openings.

Curriculum Vitaes...

The purpose of your CV is to get you invited to an interview – it is an advertisement for yourself, so spending a bit of extra time on its preparation is a good investment. As you go through university, bear in mind that having a balance of activities and experiences will reflect well on your CV so try and get involved in things that'll look impressive to a potential employer

Make the most of university facilities: try and be computer-literate by the time you graduate; be up-to date with the latest technology; or take advantage of the language labs and learn a new language.

Extra curricular activities

There are hundreds of opportunities to develop your CV at university so look out for activities that show you have team skills like playing for a team or acting in a play. Leadership qualities are also important and these can be gained by taking on positions such as being on the student council or PR for the sailing club.

Degree skills

Even your subject of study gives you relevant skills, so work out what they are and how they could be applied to the job you are going for. Your course may include presentations, research skills, group work, lab practicals or problem solving. Even if you have studied history and you decide to apply for a job in Marketing, you can employ the research skills you have developed during your degree to market research. It is useful to make a list of all the skills you have learnt and then pick out the ones you could apply to your chosen job.

Preparing your Curriculum Vitae

There are a variety of ways to write your CV, but we suggest a chronological CV which more traditional employees prefer. You may choose another format, but bear in mind the points included.

Personal Information

Name	Emma Carr
Address	19 Woodshaft Avenue, Hampshire, BH24 4FR
Contact Nos	Home - (01234) 567891
	Mobile - 07770 123456
	E-mail - xxxx@Hotmail.com
Marital Status	Single
Date of birth	07.08.79
Other	Non-smoker, good health, clean driving licence.

Education and Qualifications

1998 – 2001 **University of Wales, Cardiff**
BA English Literature (Class 2.2)
Modules included Language in the Business
Industry and Creative Writing.

1996 – 1998 **St Peter's Sixth Form, Bournemouth**
3 'A' Levels: English Literature (A), History (B),
French (B)
Duke of Edinburgh awards: bronze, silver and
gold.

1991 – 1996   **Fernhill Manor School, New Milton**
8 GCSEs: English Literature (A*), English
Language (A*), History (A), Maths (B), French
(B), Biology (B), Chemistry (C), Music (C).

Career History/Work Experience

1999 – 2001   **Bar Med, Cardiff**
Bar work
◆ Implemented two new themed nights in bar
◆ Responsible for training new staff

June 1998   **New Book Publishers, London**
Work Experience (2 weeks)
◆ Worked well as part of a team on a book launch
under considerable pressure.
◆ Various administrative duties including: typing
memos, e-mails, faxes and answering phones.

1996 – 1998   **Progress Accountancy Recruitment agency,
Bournemouth**
Office junior
◆ Assisted with sorting and processing payroll.
◆ Implemented new filing system.

Interests

Canoeing: Organised three canoeing expeditions whilst a member of the university canoeing society.

Horse Riding: Ridden at a competitive level in one-day-events, both independently and as a team member.

Journalism: Written for our local paper (Bournemouth Echo) and the Cardiff Student paper (Gair Rhydd), namely in the News and Features section.

Skills

◆ Good writing skills and command of English language.
◆ Proven ability to work as part of a team, or independently.
◆ Good conversational and written French.
◆ Experience of a range of word-processing, spreadsheets, database and statistical computer packages.

Referees

Dr S White   Mr Sandham
School of English   Manager of NBP
Cardiff University   17 Soho Square
CF24 3AT   London
                                WID 5HG

Personal Tutor   Work Experience Supervisor

CV tips

◆ It is best to confine your CV to 2 pages.
◆ Always have the CV typed on good quality A4 white paper.
◆ Do not use a fancy folder/binder and don't waste a page with just your name on the front.
◆ Use short, well-spaced paragraphs with emphasis on being concise and factual.
◆ Always proof read your CV to make sure it is error free.
◆ Give each of your referees a copy of your CV.
◆ Never give reasons for leaving a job on your CV as it could seem negative.
◆ Don't use exact dates. Months and years are sufficient.

Covering Letters

All CVs need a covering letter which again should be word-processed. This will be the first thing the employer sees so it is essential it makes a good impression.

◆ Try and find out the name of the person receiving your CV so you can personalise the letter.
◆ Use one side of A4 paper.
◆ State the post you are applying for and where you saw it advertised.
◆ Say enthusiastically why you are interested in the position.

- Refer to relevant skills and/or experience you have to offer which can provide a direct benefit to the employer.
- Close the letter indicating your availability for interview and showing optimism that you will be called for interview e.g. 'I look forward to hearing from you'.
- Start with 'Dear Mr Andrews' and end with 'Yours sincerely'. (If you haven't found out who to address the letter to, start with 'Dear Sir/Madam' and close with 'Yours faithfully').

The Successful Interviewee

Before the day of the interview:

1 Research:

Find out as much information about the company as possible:
a) Research libraries/databases/websites for information regarding the company.
b) Talk to friends/colleagues who may know the company.
c) Thoroughly read any job descriptions/newspaper advertisements.

2 Preparation:

a) Check/confirm date, time and location of interview.

b) Ensure you know the name/title of the person/people you will be meeting.

c) Plan to arrive 10 minutes early.

d) Decide on any key questions that you want to ask at interview – prioritise these and make a list e.g:

- ◆ What are the main responsibilities/duties?
- ◆ What career development/training opportunities are available?

e) Think about the image you want to create – decide what is appropriate to wear.

3 On the day:

- ◆ Be smart and well presented.
- ◆ Be punctual – arrive with time to spare.
- ◆ Travel light – don't carry a huge rucksack or your shopping.
- ◆ On arrival, be polite and pleasant to all staff you encounter (smile). Look and listen to get a feel for the organisation.

4 Create a good first impression:

This might seem obvious – but it cannot be overstated - an interviewer will begin forming an opinion of you from the minute you arrive.

- ◆ Remember to smile.
- ◆ A firm handshake is essential as it suggests a positive/confident attitude.

- Be aware of your body language (adopt an upright, but fairly relaxed position). It is worth noting that people remember:

    7% of words spoken

    38% of your voice tone

    55% of body language such as mannerisms, posture and eye contact.
- Maintain eye contact with the interviewer (look – don't stare!).
- Expect to do most of the talking.
- Communicate clearly and concisely – don't ramble.
- Be honest – don't exaggerate (you wouldn't want the interviewer to).
- Listen carefully as it shows interest and an ability to concentrate.
- Stress your strengths, achievements and ambitions – especially if related to the job/company.
- Make sure you ask all the relevant questions.
- Express a definite interest in the company and position.
- Above all – be enthusiastic.

"I remember sitting outside the interview room. I was so nervous that my hands were shaking and my palms were sweaty. Suddenly, to my horror, I noticed a large dollop of toothpaste on my jacket. This didn't do much for my nerves, but I suppose at least they knew I cleaned my teeth."

5 Leave a good lasting impression:

(a) Give a firm handshake.

(b) Maintain eye contact.

(c) Confirm your interest in the position.

(d) Say 'thank you for taking the time to see me'.

6 Possible questions asked at interview:

- ◆ Will you please give me a brief summary of your work experience?
- ◆ Why did you decide to leave the job?
- ◆ How do you feel about working long hours/weekends?
- ◆ Have you any hobbies?
- ◆ What are your greatest strengths and weaknesses?
- ◆ Do you prefer working independently or as part of a team?
- ◆ Where do you see yourself in 5 years' time?
- ◆ Why should we employ you?

UNIVERSITY CAREERS SERVICES

The majority of universities offer a free careers service to their students. It is a good idea to visit yours as they can give you various help and advice on:

◆ What career direction to take.

◆ Work placements.

◆ Work experience.

◆ Job hunting and potential employees.

◆ Help and advice with CVs and interviews.

"I didn't have a clue what direction to go in after I graduated so I visited our careers office. They were fantastic and spent a lot of time with me discussing my options and sorting out work experience. They even helped me sort out my CV and as a result I've been offered several interviews."

DIARY OF A STUDENT

After graduating from Swansea University, I soon realised that apart from my degree and a couple of summer jobs, the content of my CV was seriously lacking credibility. If you find yourself in a similar predicament, do not despair, as with a little creativity and exaggeration almost anybody's CV can become respectable (or so I thought). I followed the advice that writing your CV is your chance to show a prospective employer that you are the best person for the job and consequently it is not a situation where modesty is rewarded. As my exaggeration took momentum I found myself liking the 'new me'. I never realised I was capable of so much - Head boy at Sixth form, a member of the Equal Opportunities Council and Chairman of the University Tennis Club. I was a busy guy.

The CV worked a treat and I got my first interview with an investment-banking firm in London. The interview began well as I arrived punctually, looking smart and sophisticated and gave the firm handshake I'd been coached to use. Unfortunately things took a turn for the worst when I was asked about the duties involved in my Equal Opportunities position. It soon became painfully clear that I was not quite in the know about women's rights or racial policies as my dazzling CV began to unravel at the seams. After a very awkward 20 minutes, I left the interview with a rather red face and needless to say didn't get offered the job.

Matt Clarke, *Graduate of European Business Studies*

CHAPTER 8

RECIPES

It's easy to fall into bad eating habits at university – mum's not there to have dinner waiting on the table when you get in, Tesco seems like a long way away when it's raining and the Chinese take-away looks kind of tempting...

A Balanced Diet

Eating a balanced diet is essential to good health. A healthy diet should contain a variety of nutrients – protein, carbohydrates, fat, vitamins and minerals and fibre. On the whole we tend to eat too much fat, salt and sugar and not enough fibre.

A diet which is high in fat, especially saturated fat, increases blood cholesterol levels, thereby increasing the risk of coronary heart disease. This does not mean you should cut fats out of your diet, rather eat them in moderation. Choose semi-skimmed milk instead of full-fat, low fat cheeses, lean meat, and go easy on the chocolate and cakes.

Sugar contains "empty calories", i.e. it provides energy but contains no nutrients. It is best to eat foods such as fruit and vegetables for energy, which also provide vitamins and minerals. Alcohol contains many "empty calories," so watch out or that beer-belly will start to set in.

Fibre is an essential part of our diet because it plays an important role in our digestive systems. A lack of fibre can lead to constipation and bowel problems. You can increase the fibre in your diet by eating wholemeal bread, pasta, rice and flour rather than white.

"When I got home at Christmas no-one recognised me – the pints, kebabs and chips were finally taking their toll in the shape of an enormous beer gut. For my New Year's resolution I decided to learn how to cook."

Basic ingredients to stock in your cupboards

Carbohydrates	Dairy	Vegetables	Seasoning
pasta	milk	peppers	salt
rice	eggs	lettuce	pepper
bread	butter	cucumber	dried herbs e.g. basil
potatoes	cheese	onions	tomato sauce
		mushrooms	soy sauce
			sugar

These are some of the basics that allow you to make anything from scrambled egg to extravagant pasta dishes.

Breakfast ideas

Breakfast is renowned to be the most important meal of the day because it gives you a kick start and sets you up for the rest of the day.

- ◆ **Cereals** such as Cornflakes or Weetabix can be spruced up with:
  - dried apricots/raisins
  - almonds
  - chopped banana on top.

◆ **Yoghurts** – again try adding some chopped fruit and nuts to yoghurts to boost your vitamin and mineral intake.

◆ **Eggs** are a nutritious way to start the day if you are feeling adventurous. Try them scrambled, boiled, poached or fried (see below).

Eggs

Soft boiled egg

Place eggs into a saucepan of simmering water.
Bring to the boil and then simmer for 4 minutes.
Remove the egg and slice the top off with a knife.

Fried egg

Heat oil in a frying pan until foaming, then crack the egg into the pan. Fry for 3-4 minutes, spooning hot oil over the yolk until the egg has completely whitened.

Scrambled egg

Beat 2 eggs together in a bowl with a little milk and salt and pepper.
Melt a small knob of butter in a pan, then pour in the eggs.
Cook on a low heat until thickened, stirring continuously.
(You can also cook scrambled egg in the microwave on full power for 2 minutes.)

Poached egg

Heat a saucepan of water until simmering then crack the egg into the water.

Leave to cook for approximately 3 minutes until whitened.

Lift the egg out with a big spoon.

French Omelette

Ingredients:
2 large eggs
knob of butter
drop of water
fresh herbs
salt and pepper

Method:
Beat the eggs, herbs and seasoning together. Heat the butter in a frying pan.

Pour the eggs into the pan and leave to set for approximately 5 minutes, stirring occasionally.

Tasty Variations:
Try adding any of the following ingredients:

◆ cheese
◆ chopped tomatoes and bacon
◆ spinach and mushroom.

Lunch ideas

- **Beans on toast** – you can't go wrong with these. Try a few variations on the theme:
    - Spread marmite on the toast
    - Add grated cheese on top
    - Spread soft cheese on your bread.

- **Toasties** – Someone usually brings a sandwich toaster to uni and they are ideal when lunching at home. Try some of these combo's:
    - cheese and tomato ketchup
    - bacon and egg
    - ham, cheese and tomato
    - turkey slices and onion.

- **Sandwiches** – if you often eat lunch on the go, save yourself some money and take sandwiches with you. Use different types of bread to vary your daily diet:
    - pittas
    - bagels
    - baguettes
    - brown/white sliced bread
    - ciabatta bread.

Mix and match with a selection of fillings:

- coleslaw, celery and cheddar
- brie and bacon
- cottage cheese and dried apricot
- ham and mustard
- cheese and marmite.

Dinner ideas

(All recipes serve 1 unless otherwise stated)

Pasta

Creamy Cheesy Pasta

Ingredients:
100g pasta
20g butter
25g Parmesan cheese
70ml cream
Chopped fresh herbs

Method:
Cook the pasta in a saucepan of water until soft.
Melt the butter in a saucepan on a low heat.

Stir in the Parmesan and cream and bring to the boil, then simmer until the sauce thickens.

Remove from the heat and add the herbs and seasoning if required.

Mix the sauce in with the pasta.

Napolitana

Ingredients:
100g pasta
1 tbsp olive oil
1 onion, finely chopped
1 can chopped tomatoes
pinch of fresh herbs

Method:
Cook the pasta in a saucepan of water until soft.

Fry the onion in the oil until brown and softened.

Stir in the chopped tomatoes and herbs.

Bring to the boil and then reduce the heat and simmer until thickened.

Mix the sauce into the pasta.

Add grated cheese on top for extra taste.

White Sauce

This is a great base for many dishes such as lasagne, macaroni cheese, fish pie, cauliflower cheese, vegetable crumble etc.

Ingredients:
40g butter
40g plain flour
600ml hot milk

Method:
Heat the butter in a saucepan until melted. Stir in the flour and then the milk. Whisk on a medium heat until thickened. You can season with salt, pepper or spices.

Meat

Stir-fries

Basic Ingredients:
Sauce (see below)
100g boneless chicken breast or pork
1 tbsp oil
1 onion, finely chopped
$^1/_2$ pepper, cut into sticks

3 small mushrooms, sliced

sweetcorn

1 carrot, peeled and thinly sliced

25g beansprouts

(You can choose from the above vegetables depending on your tastes and what you've got in the cupboard.)

Method:

Heat the oil in a frying pan.

Place chicken in frying pan with the onion. Fry until brown.

Add the pepper, mushrooms, carrot and beansprouts, stirring continuously for 3 – 4 minutes.

Continue stirring and add the sauce.

Serve with rice or noodles.

Stir-fry sauces

Mix together the following ingredients for different variations of stir-fry. You can use pork, beef, fish or prawns instead of the chicken.

◆ **Lemon and ginger**

Juice of half a lemon

2cm of fresh ginger, finely chopped

1 tbsp soy sauce

◆ Sweet and sour
1 tbsp cornflour
1 tbsp soy sauce
1 tbsp orange juice
1 tsp sugar

◆ Oriental
$1/2$ a garlic clove, crushed
$1/2$ tsp curry powder
$1/2$ tsp chilli powder
1 tbsp soy sauce

Chilli con Carne
(Serves 2)

Ingredients:
200g minced beef
1 tbsp oil
1 onion, chopped
1 garlic clove, crushed
1 tsp chilli powder
1 tin chopped tomatoes
1 tin kidney beans, drained
1 tsp sugar
$1/2$ tsp salt

Method:

Fry the onion and garlic in oil until softened.

Add the mince and fry until it browns.

Stir in the chopped tomatoes, sugar, salt and chilli powder.

Simmer gently for an hour, stirring occasionally.

Approximately 15 minutes before the end add the kidney beans.

(To bulk up for unexpected guests, add a tin of baked beans.)

You can use this chilli recipe in lasagnes, cottage pie, in tortillas or served with rice or spaghetti.

Potatoes

Jacket Potatoes

Cheap, quick, healthy and very easy - the staple student diet. There are loads of simple different variations you can try to make life a little more interesting...

◆ Cheese and beans
◆ Tuna and sweetcorn
◆ Cream cheese and bacon
◆ Chicken, salad and mayonnaise
◆ Guacamole and salsa
◆ Prawn and mayonnaise
◆ Cheese, ham and pineapple.

Potato Bake

Ingredients:
150g potatoes, peeled and sliced
Small knob of butter
150ml milk
1 onion peeled and sliced
50g cheese, grated
salt & pepper

Method:
Heat the oven and grease a shallow dish.
Layer potatoes, onion, cheese and seasoning, finishing with a layer of potatoes.
Pour milk over top and dot remaining butter over top.
Bake for about $1^{1}/_{2}$ hrs or until tender. Serve with tomatoes and green salad.

Pudding Ideas

If you ever treat yourself to puddings or cook for your friends, a simple, cheap yummy pudding can be made using vanilla ice-cream and adding bits on top such as:

◆ crushed Dime bar
◆ melted mint chocolate
◆ Baileys
◆ crushed Crunchie bar
◆ crumbled flake.

Other Useful Student Books from How To Books

A-Z of Correct English, Angela Burt, 2000

Critical Thinking for Students, Roy van den Brink-Budgen, 2000

CVs for Graduates, Gerald Higginbottom, 2001

Handling Tough Job Interviews, Julie-Ann Amos, 2001

Improving Your Written English, Marion Field, 1998

The Internet Job Search Handbook, Andrea Semple and Matt Haigue, 2001

Make Exams Easy, Mike Evans, 2001

Passing Exams Without Anxiety, David Acres, 1998

Polish up Your Punctuation and Grammar, Marion Field, 2000

Read Faster, Recall More, Gordon Wainwright, 2001

Worldwide Volunteering for Young People, 3rd edition 2001

Writing an Essay, Brendan Hennessy, 1997

Writing Successful Essays, Brendan Hennessy, 2000

Write a Winning CV, Julie-Ann Amos, 2001

For comprehensive information on How To Books titles visit
How To Books on-line at **www.howtobooks.co.uk**

List of Useful Web Sites

General Student Websites
www.juiced.co.uk
www.virginstudent.com
www.studentsgetoff.com

National Union of Students: student life and welfare matters:
www.nusonline.co.uk/

National Union of Students Northern Ireland: student life and welfare matters:
www.nistudents.com/

London students
www.londonstudent.org.uk

UCAS (Universities & Colleges Admissions Service for the UK)
www.ucas.com

Online guide for PUSH Guide to Which Universities
www.push.co.uk

Information on going to uni.
www.infoyouth.com

Health
www.studenthealth.co.uk

Buying and selling textbooks
www.swotbooks.com

Year in Industry
www.yini.org.uk

Student Volunteering
www.studentvol.org.uk
www.worldwidevolunteering.org.uk

Travel & Vacation Work
www.howtobooks.co.uk
www.statravel.co.uk
www.campamerica.co.uk
www.thegapyear.co.uk
www.gap.org.uk
www.bunac.org

We Want Your Feedback

Remember, this book was written by students for students. But we won't be staying students forever! So send us your own ideas and suggestions for possible inclusion in the *Guide*.

Everyone who writes to us c/o our publishers and has their suggestions included in the next edition will find their name in it, too. The best contributions will get a free copy sent to the contributor.

Send all correspondence to:

Student Survival Guide
How To Books Ltd
3 Newtec Place
Magdalen Road
Oxford
OX4 1RE

or e-mail us at **studentsurvival@howtobooks.co.uk** or visit our website **www.studentsurvivalguide.co.uk**

Remember to include your return address – and to let us know if you *don't* want your letter published or your name acknowledged.